UNDER

UNDERSONG

LISTENING TO THE SOUL

Peter B. Price

To Peter

with best wishes

Peter P.

DARTON · LONGMAN + TODD

First published in 2002 by
Darton, Longman and Todd Ltd
1 Spencer Court
140-142 Wandsworth High Street
London SW18 4JJ

Reprinted 2002

ISBN 0–232–52440–8

A catalogue record for this book is available
from the British Library.

The Scripture quotations in this publication are taken from
The New Jerusalem Bible, published and copyright 1985 and 1990
by Darton, Longman and Todd Ltd and Doubleday and Co. Inc.

Designed by Sandie Boccacci
Phototypeset in 10/12½pt Times by
Intype London Ltd
Printed and bound in Great Britain by
The Bath Press, Bath

The *undersong* is the emotional current that carries us along through the very life of the inner world.

RALPH WALDO EMERSON

For Dee,
rich gift and companion in the *undersong* –
the pull and push of the journey.

CONTENTS

THANKS . . .

THIS IS A BOOK OF STORIES that meet up with a single story, mine. For many years now I have been collecting the tales, the insights and reflections of countless people whom I have had the privilege of meeting all over the world. Some of these are acknowledged in this book, some cannot be for a multitude of reasons, and many are not. To them all a special thankyou for the way in which their story has shaped mine and led me into new places, warned me away from dangers, and sustained me when the journey has been difficult.

Among my gurus is one in particular, Fr Pat Clarke CSSP, to whom I owe a great deal in the nearly twenty years since we met in a *favela* in São Paolo. My spiritual director, Christine Roberts, has been a constant source of inspiration and an honest friend, who, along with Canon Jeffrey John, Canon Theologian of South-wark, and Rev. Sylvia Roberts, has kindly read and guided me in the writing of the manuscript.

Most of my writing is done in the early morning, or late at night. Much of the text has been emailed in various states of incompleteness to Daphne Jowit, who has painstakingly addressed the endless grammatical, typing and other errors, as well as offering valuable suggestions for improving the text. Liz Chesman has borne the brunt of all the other office work while the last-minute attempts to meet the deadline have been tried! To both I owe my gratitude.

Liam de Frinse, one of Ireland's leading contemporary artists, has kindly provided the illustration for the cover. Being with

Liam on a Donegal seashore is to gain a whole new perspective on things, and I am grateful to him for his generosity.

I want to thank Teresa de Bertodano and Morag Reeve for their encouragement, more than ten years ago, to write this book. Brendan Walsh and other colleagues at Darton, Longman and Todd have seen it through to completion, and to them, too, I am grateful.

PETER B. PRICE
St Aidan's Day

PRELUDE – UNDERSONG

'THE UNDERSONG,' WROTE Ralph Waldo Emerson, 'is the emotional current that carries us along through the very life of the inner world.' All of us have an inner world. Here we discover our loves and our hates, our joys and sorrows, our beliefs and our unbelief. Here, too, depending on our self-awareness, we discover the 'self' and the 'God' at the core of our being. Some people call the energy of this inner life their spirituality, whether or not they give it a religious focus. I am someone who believes that the 'emotional current that carries us through the very life of the inner world' is nothing less than the Spirit of God. I have found, too, that wherever I am within the life of the inner world, God is both present and active, enabling me to discern something, not only of who God is, but of what it means to be a human being.

My spirituality has always been a matter of fits and starts. Someone[1] has expressed this as the 'yearning [which] is both the beginning and ending of the story, both the pull and push of the journey.' The term 'undersong' sums up my experience of the spiritual journey. In the journeys of my life I have met many others who also experience this 'current' or 'yearning' – within the 'pull and push' of life. Some of these have been people of public faith, others have not, but in each and all of them I have discerned something of both God and humanity. Being with others, in silence and in speech, listening to stories, observing rituals, I sense that I have touched the very life of God in a way that has offered compassion and hope.

I wrote these early words in hospital recovering from surgery. The past few years have brought me from time to time to contemplate mortality as a result of needing the attention of the surgeon's knife. The post-operative state often leaves the patient open to voices that they would not normally hear. Some of those are inner voices, words of the spirit, whether Holy or not. Other voices are those of the people around, nurses, ward orderlies, visitors, fellow patients. My time in hospital was a small window in the pull and push of my life, and in it I experienced being cared for by others, nearly all strangers, all of whom were concerned for my cure.

Thomas Moore reminds us that the Latin *cura* means 'cure of the soul', which in turn means several things: 'attention, devotion, husbandry, adorning of the body, healing, managing, being anxious for, and worshipping the gods.'[2] To be cured is not simply a question of recovering from whatever ailment has been diagnosed. To be cured is something holistic, relating to all dimensions of our life. My recuperation in hospital was subject to continuous monitoring, or 'observance'. Regularly, pulse, temperature and blood pressure were checked.

For several days the location of my bed was near the nurses' station. One day I was feeling below par, the adrenalin that had supplied me the energy to face the operation, and the relief at its success, had passed. As the day staff handed over to the night shift, I heard my condition being discussed. The clinical observations were shared, and then somewhat to my surprise I found my well-being under discussion. I was perceived as being 'not too good today', and 'a bit down'. It was true, of course, but perhaps what surprised me was the extent of the 'observance'. It made concrete for me Thomas More's reflection on the root word of observance – *serv*, which in the Latin means 'tending the sheep' or 'keeping an eye on whatever is wandering, or grazing', whether it be 'the latest addiction, a striking dream, or a troubling mood'.[3]

JOURNEYS OF THE SPIRIT

This is a book about journeys of the spirit. It is at times auto-biographical, with some 'wandering and grazing' into the experience and insights of others. It is a way-mark on a longer journey. It reflects where the emotional current of the *undersong* has led thus far. I hope it will not be too distracting. There is always a danger that those not in the first flush of youth become maudlin or moralizing, rather than seeking to do what Jung commends, namely, 'spending the second half of life – redeeming the first.' The themes of love, forgiveness, peacemaking, justice, prayer and others that this little book seeks to address are fundamental not only to the inner life of the spirit, but to the way in which we live and act in this beautiful world that has been entrusted to us.

I have always been a traveller, a journey maker. This has led to a certain restlessness with life, an all-too-frequent desire to move on, rather than to put down roots and settle. 'It's more difficult to hit a moving target,' my sons occasionally joke. But the journeying and travelling are not always comfortable in themselves. Much of journeying is waiting, and often that waiting is anxious, frustrating and occasionally frightening. My earliest recall of the travail of travel was as a three-year-old standing holding desperately to my mother's hand in the huge transit sheds at Southampton docks, waiting in a noisy sea of khaki to board a troop ship. The sense of being 'in transit' has never really left me.

There is a sort of searching, a longing for a place of safety, a harbour, in the Welsh *noddfa* – a place of refuge. When I seek to understand who God is, and who God is for me, I find that I am less dependent upon certainties, absolutes, more in search of person, personhood and relationship. It is relationship that matters, rather than places and policies. My spiritual director once remarked about ministry that she believed, 'We only go into all this because we need all this . . .' I hope in some sense this book will help people like me who are in this journey of the spirit to understand not only that 'we need all this' but *why* we need it.

It is the nature of being in transit, or on a journey, that it takes time to see the end from the beginning. On a journey many conversations are held. As Reuben Alves has observed, 'a complete sentence kills the conversation dead. An incomplete sentence keeps the conversation going.' Journeying is not for those who like things nicely sorted, those who must have their opinions formed, their dogma determined. Journeying is for those who recognize that they will have to cross boundaries, borders, and in crossing them risk conversion to people, insights and purposes beyond their securities and safety.

CROSSING BOUNDARIES

Travelling some years ago through Tanzania I read a book that, despite my best endeavours to return to it, has never given me the same insight as it did during that journey. It was Marcel Möring's *The Great Longing*. He told familiar stories, many of which he had culled from other writers. One of these is about the Rabbi Meir, a great sage and saint.

> The rabbi took lessons from a heretic, Elisha ben Abiyuh, who was called Akher, the Stranger. One Saturday Rabbi Meir was out with his teacher and they got involved in a deep discussion. The teacher was riding a donkey, and the rabbi, who was not allowed to ride on a Saturday, walked beside him. He was listening so intently to his teacher that he didn't realize they had reached the ritual boundary, which the Jews were not allowed to cross on the Sabbath. His teacher pointed this out to him. He said, 'This is where we must part – you may not accompany me any further. Go back.' So Rabbi Meir turned back, while his teacher rode on beyond the boundaries of the Jewish community.[4]

There is a paradox in this story. We cross boundaries almost before we are aware of them. Birth is our first and perhaps most profound crossing, and death our last and most mysterious. The whole of our human journey is made crossing boundaries and borders. Most of them we scarcely notice, though who of us forgets the border crossing of approaching our first love? Such journeys carry with them both desire and foreboding. In essence it is a reaching out to something or someone else. In all such crossings we risk hurt and hope: the possibility of being changed. We experience a form of education, from the Latin *educare* – a leading out, a learning from others, from circumstances and situations that are almost subliminal. 'I did learn what I didn't know I wanted to know,' says one of my gurus.[5]

DISCOVERING FIDELITY

For many years I have kept a Commonplace Book. In its earliest incarnation it was more a diary of the spirit than a source of reflection. Returning to some of the early writings is at times embarrassing and humbling, and I am enormously tempted to throw them out – and hope that maybe before I die I will have the strength to light one more bonfire! I like to think that the reflections written in recent years are more mature and sophisticated. The truth, I suspect, is that these more contemporary observations have included more self-consciously the experience of others both through direct encounter and writings. What keeps me from throwing away the earlier reflections is that they reveal what is an ongoing truth about who I am, namely one for whom the journey to wholeness remains difficult. I admit to this because I sense that it is true for most of us. Also, the very fitfulness of things reveals for me a deeper truth, that despite all my fickleness, when I recover a measure of consistency in my relationship with who God is for me, I discover a fidelity, a faithfulness in the One I all too fitfully seek.

On my first Ignatian retreat, my director invited me to begin with time contemplating three questions: 'Where are you?' 'What are you doing here?' 'Who are you looking for?' The first of these questions, 'Where are you?', was asked by God of Adam in the Garden of Eden story. The second, 'What are you doing here?', of Elijah hiding in his cave following the defeat of the prophets of Baal. The third, 'Who are you looking for?', was asked of the seekers who came looking for Jesus. They were searching and ultimately revealing questions, but they were coupled with two verses from Isaiah: 'Your salvation lay in conversion and tranquillity, your strength in serenity and trust and you would have none of it. But Yahweh is waiting to be gracious to you, the Exalted One, to take pity on you.'[6]

Discovering where we are in the journey of the spirit is important, if we are in some measure to discover our vocation, our calling – what we are doing here. Integral to the questions is relationship – 'Who are you looking for?' For the past forty or so years I have sought to be in relationship with God through the person of Jesus Christ, who seems to me to provide the most complete insight and understanding of the nature of God. It has been an experience of conversion, a conversion that 'is both a distinct moment and a continuous process', as Orlando Costas has put it. And, as my late but good friend Guillermo Cook used to say, 'When we are converted to Christ, we are converted to God *and* to humanity.'[7]

Conversion to humanity is integral to the *undersong*. Jesus urged people 'not to worry about your life'.[8] In our world far too many are anxious. Without conversion towards such people, our belief that 'the God who gives daily bread will meet all basic needs if people are faithful and just', will be empty.[9] The *undersong* must sooner or later lead us to the boundaries of our 'self' and require us either to retreat into individualism and uncritical piety, or to contemplate the 'other': God, community, the self beyond self.

Tranquillity, serenity and trust are concepts that too often get tied into a spirituality that avoids the realities of our world. True tranquillity is that which is achieved when we face the addictions, dreams, moods, avoidances that prevent us from being fully human. In my journey I have discovered that where the big issues of life confront the need for forgiveness, reconciliation, or peace-making, there is a purpose of God to be found. When we allow those realities to be part of the inner life of the spirit, then we lay ourselves open to the possibility of discovering the serenity and trust that God so desires for his people.

In a sense this vignette from my retreat sums up for me the paradox of the *undersong*. There are times when the possibility of salvation, which I take to mean health, wholeness, tranquillity and serenity, together with trust, lies open for us. There are times too when we jettison this possibility in favour of other illusions, other securities. Yet the mysterious Divine is the ever-present emotional current, constantly washing, like the tide, towards grace and hope.

I have written *Undersong* in different places – at home in suburban London, in Donegal, in the north-west of Ireland. Many of the sources have been penned in places as varied as early post-apartheid South Africa, war-torn El Salvador, and post-Mao China. It is a collection of stories that have influenced and made my story. *Undersong* is that emotion which touches all of us in our journey from wherever we begin to travel.

Throughout the writing of this book, people have asked, 'Who is it for?' I have replied, 'I hope it is for people who are spiritual, but who do not think they are Christian; and for people who are Christian, but do not consider themselves to be spiritual.' What I mean is that spirituality is about the whole of our lives, the ordinary and the extraordinary, the public and the private. Spirituality touches the intimacy of the personal, and nurtures the courage of witness, the possibility of the prophetic. It is the conscious and unconscious act of listening to the soul, and in it discerning the authentic voice of God. Whether this book has achieved that is a matter for discovery. It is a reflection of the life of the spirit, sometimes with a capital 'S'. But whether upper or lower case is used to describe the Spirit, I am in little doubt that it is God as Source of all being, Eternal Word, and Holy Spirit who is the emotional current that carries us along, as well as being the beginning and the ending of the story.

1

THE UNDERSONG
OF THE CHILD WITHIN

I OCCASIONALLY TAKE A TAXI in London where I live. I enjoy
chatting to taxi drivers, who nearly always have a wry view of life
at street level. Some cabbies, however, are more of a challenge
than others. Nothing, it seems, will get them talking. I rode with
one such person recently, but because the traffic was so bad, and
the fare was going to be astronomic for the distance travelled, the
ice melted and he spoke. It was like turning on a fountain! He
told me all about his life, about his search for God – but his failure
so far to find him; the frailty of his wife, his unfaithfulness – and
the litany went on.

At my destination I paid my fare. I put my head through the
window to say goodbye when he blurted out, 'I sometimes
wonder if I have ever been loved.' Much to my surprise he picked
up a Bible from the floor of his cab. He continued, 'I try to read
this to find out, but I guess I've made such a mess of things . . .' –
and he trailed into silence. I took the Bible from him and found
him some words from the opening chapter of the prophet Jeremiah, 'Before I formed you in the womb I knew you, I filled you
with potential.' I said, 'God has loved you, like he loved Jeremiah,
before you were ever a gleam in your mother's eye. And God still
does.' His face lit up, some tears came to his eyes, and he shook
my hand and drove off smiling.

I don't know who was the more gob-smacked, as my children
say; but I realized that I had shared with him a truth that I find
increasingly significant: that to know oneself loved, whether by

God or one's fellow human beings, is the greatest need of human-kind. The concept of being 'known' in the Scriptures is profound; it incorporates not only the sense that one who is 'known' has both worth and potential, but that they are also loved. And in that being loved there is an even deeper truth, that though the one who is being loved may not be able to comprehend it, the one who is loving – God – loves for God's sake too. I take this to mean that in the very act of loving, God, and any other who loves, does so in order to give authenticity to their own personhood.

BEING NAMED

In my early days as a secondary school teacher I was often asked to speak at the school assembly. We'd had a run of teenage pregnancies, and welfare officers and the curriculum staff sought ways of improving sex education and advice over contraception. Christmas was coming, and I was asked to speak at the school carol service. I'd been reading some of the writings of Paul Tournier, a Swiss psychiatrist, who was described on the book jackets as 'a man skilled in medicine and wise towards God'. He recounted a consultation with a pregnant teenager who had come to ask a fellow consultant to help her have an abortion. Justifying her request, she said to the doctor, 'After all, doctor, it's not all that important! It's only a little bundle of cells!' Unjudgementally, the consultant asked that young mother one small question: 'If you were to keep your baby, what name would you give it?' There was a long silence. Then suddenly the woman rose and said, 'Thank you, doctor, I'll keep it.'

The consultant recounting the story observed that 'during that long silence, I was watching that young woman . . . I had a feeling I was witnessing the birth of the person of her child . . . It was no longer a "little bundle of cells" – it was a living person entrusted to her love.'[1]

I decided to tell this story as I introduced the Christmas story at the carol service. Afterwards several of the senior girls came and thanked me for it, telling me that it had moved them and made them think.

There is a grace in being named. When I was a parish priest, I recall a woman who suffered a great deal, was constantly in and out of hospital, yet somehow it became apparent that her physical illness was linked to some deeper emotional disorder. Visiting her one afternoon, she told me that she had had an abortion many years ago and had been unable to forgive herself. We talked a little about the circumstances, and the reasons she had made the decision. Then I remembered Tournier's story. Gently I asked her if she would like to name the child. She too thought awhile. Not knowing the gender, she thought of a name that would cover both. It was Francis, or Frances. We prayed, and thanked God for the life held in another place and time. She told me subsequently that the naming 'ceremony' had released something in her that enabled her to deal with her physical disabilities in a new way, and though she has never been what I would call well, she has experienced a measure of inner healing.

Many of the young people I meet here in South London have their family origins in Africa or Asia. When I baptize or confirm them, I will be given a name that comes from their birth language. I often ask, 'What does your name mean?' The replies are unfailingly beautiful, and descriptions like 'precious', 'God's own', 'chosen', or 'fragrant', 'joyful', 'serene', and many more, are offered. It is often in the grace of naming that we find something of the dreams our parents had for us. My wife's birth name means 'rich gift'. I can bear testimony to the truth of that for our relationship, but my mother-in-law tells me that she chose it because as a child there was a particularly elegant and beautiful woman in her village called Edith, and she was the inspiration for the naming!

We have been blessed with four sons, and when I reflect on their respective personalities and listen to the *undersong* that has revealed who they are today, I see a remarkable coincidence between name and person. David, 'the man of love', or 'the one after God's own heart', is one of the most sensitive and thoughtful young people I have known. Patrick, his brother, besides being named after the patron saint of Ireland, has a name that means 'noble'. Patrick is a person of the most enormous integrity, a real man of his word. Neil, occupying that unenviable third place, has a name that means 'champion'. When he was nine years old we bought Neil a poster that has a pile of oranges topped by an onion. The slogan read, 'You don't get to the top by being the same as everybody else'. Despite its obvious ambivalence, it was to encourage him to believe in his uniqueness. He is now a gifted teacher, a loved and true 'champion' of and among his pupils. John, our eleven-year 'after-thought', means 'God is gracious'. In him we have observed graces of warmth, support, humanity and courage, and as we anticipate his leaving home, we have come to realize how much his name sums up what we feel about him and the others – 'God is gracious'.

THE MYSTERY, GRACE, AND HOPE OF BEING LOVED

I suppose each of us, like the cab driver I mentioned earlier, has wondered whether we 'have ever been loved'. Our hectic life-styles leave us all too little time for contemplation. Their very busyness seems almost a running away from the possibility of loving and being loved. The materialism of our times offers the possibility of many love substitutes. Discerning how God loves, and is gracious, is for most people an unrecognized *undersong*. Yet it is often in childhood that people have their most profound and close encounters with God. Dan Millman[2] gives a particularly poignant example. He writes about Sachi, who asked her parents to leave her alone with her new baby brother. Eventually the parents agreed, and sitting quietly outside a partly opened door, 'they saw little Sachi walk quietly up to her baby brother, put her face close to his and say quietly, "Baby, tell me what God feels like. I'm starting to forget." '

Deeply hidden within our psyche is something of the mystical relationship with the Other, the Creator. My wife recalls how one Sunday, while sitting in church at the age of three, she had a profound sense of the goodness of God, and of God's love for her. Many of us may not be able to recall such an experience, nor be able to articulate it, or even call it to mind, but within us all there is a deep longing to be loved, to be valued, to be found to be of value. Those who seek a spirituality based on the practice of St Ignatius are advised in their first retreat that they cannot move

on into the 'spiritual exercises' until they have come to a point of
acceptance within themselves that they are loved by God for who
they are. Moments of disclosure cannot be predicted, of course,
and yet it is surprising that when we put ourselves in the way of
their possibility, they have a remarkable habit of occurring.

> Once a little boy was trying to open a flower bud. Under
> his persistent efforts the blossom fell apart in his hands. In
> exasperation he looked up at his mother and asked, "Why
> does the bud fall apart when I try to open it, but when God
> opens it the flower is beautiful?"
>
> Shocked at his profundity, his mother was speechless.
> Soon, however, the child exclaimed eagerly, "Oh, I know!
> When God opens the flower, he opens it up from the
> inside."[3]

Marva Dawn, whose story this is, remarks, 'That story is a
charming illustration of the difference between being conformed
and being transformed.' For me, it is a story that exposes the
profound truth that the child is often the most open conduit to
receiving and expressing God's love and grace. When we take
time to observe, and listen to the voice of little ones, we find
ourselves in touch with mystery, grace and hope.

My own childhood was neither particularly happy nor unhappy.
We moved house a lot, and my parents, though never poor,
belonged to that kind of permanently pinched middle-class group
for whom money was always an anxiety, and the desire for fulfilment of their own thwarted ambitions in their children almost
overbearing. There was a lot of control, fear, anger and the
resentment that springs from believing in one's own intellectual
superiority, but at the same time being grudging that it has not
earned the economic well-being of those less intellectually
endowed.

There was love, of course. Christmas was always a sort of
'making up' time. Every care was taken to ensure surprise and, as
far as money allowed, the provision of presents that were wanted.
It seemed that Christmas, and to a lesser extent birthdays, provided the opportunity for expressing tangibly what had not been
able to be expressed through touch, or time taken to listen. Our

family history remained a mystery, neither parent able to talk about themself and their relationship to their parents.

It was one of those serendipitous moments many years later that brought me to an understanding of the paradox of fear and love in my parents. During the late seventies, with our young family we lived for a while in the Yorkshire Dales. One late October my parents visited us, in what was to turn out to be the last year they enjoyed free of ill health. Ever watchful of wasting money, particularly on postage, they had purchased and brought with them presents for Christmas. We stored them on the top of our bedroom wardrobe, out of reach, if not out of sight of increasingly excited children.

About two weeks before Christmas it snowed. The remoteness of our house meant that we rarely closed the bedroom curtains, and I awoke one morning to the winter light and first signs of a watery sun shining, its reflection from the snow bathing the Christmas gifts in a translucent light. I felt a sudden inexplicable surge of love for my Dad and Mum. It was far greater than any feeling of affection that I had ever had for them. Getting up, I wandered up through the snow to my office and wrote a letter to them. I told them that I loved them. I told my Dad in particular that he had the capacity to be a cantankerous old so and so, but that somehow that was all right, and that I thought I had begun to understand that much of his anger was born out of fear from unresolved things in his own life, and some of it for us, his children.

I posted the letter, feeling in my self a sense of completeness, a sort of restoration. I did not know how my Dad in particular would receive it. The next day the phone rang. It was my father. I was surprised, because he didn't make long distance phone calls. He thanked me for the letter, and greatly out of character talked away on the phone heedless of the expense! It was undoubtedly important to him, and although our relationship continued to have its ups and downs, I found the letter when I was clearing the house after his death: it was held in a small bundle of other intimate letters, chiefly from my mother.

In one sense, little changed. Touch remained taboo; there was no saying 'sorry', or 'I love you'. But there was a knowing.

Wounds had been healed. I saw the man, and he me. I think that Robert Bly has a handle on some of this when he says, ' . . . where a man's wound is, that is where his genius will be. Wherever the wound appears in our psyches, whether from an alcoholic father, shaming mother, shaming father, whether it is from isolation, disability or disease, that is precisely the place from which we will give our major gift to the community.'[4]

I do not know what my father's 'wound' was. What I do know was that in parenting terms he was passive for the most part, used more often as threat – poor man – than resource. If 'parenting means feeling, but also means doing lots of boring tasks, taking the kids to school, buying them jackets, attending band concerts, dealing with curfews, setting rules of behaviour, deciding on response when rules are broken, checking on who a child's friends are, listening to a child's talk in an active way',[5] and so on, then he didn't parent. In some sense for me that has been a wound, and I, who have been the father of four sons, have endeavoured to make up that lack with my own children. But it is in the nature of things that I will have failed them somewhere, and they too will carry wounds.

THE GOD WHO IS FOR US

When I think of my father, and I do so most days, I have found a deeper understanding, not so much of what or who he was, but of how he felt about things. Robert Bly speaks of his relationship with his father, however, in ways that I too understand. 'Every time I see my father,' he recalls, 'I have complicated and new feelings about how much of the deprivation I felt with him came willingly, and how much against his will – how much he was aware of and unaware of.'[6]

In the Jewish Christian tradition much is made of the father-hood of God. Many theologians, particularly feminist writers, have struggled with this paternalistic view of God, and have sought other paradigms from the Scriptures to accommodate the idea of intimacy without using the term 'father' – or even its more intimate form *Abba*, better translated as 'Daddy'! Terms such as crafts-person, conversationalist, deserted spouse, risk taker are certainly among the many good and accurate descriptions of who God is for us.

Jim Cotter in his 'Night Prayer' offers an alternative introduction to the Lord's Prayer as follows:

> Eternal Spirit
> Life Giver, Pain Bearer, Love Maker
> Source of all that is and that shall be,
> Father and Mother of us all
>   Loving God in whom is heaven . . . [7]

I am still agnostic about the need for change, though I acknowledge that because of the profound and deep emotions stirred in the concept of parenthood, true intimacy and understanding of the mystery of who God is for us, or would be for us, can be blurred. At the same time, there is within our perception of who God is, that which calls for a recognition of our wounds, and divine healing activity.

Some years ago I made my first of many visits to Ellis Island in New York harbour. From the late nineteenth until the middle of the twentieth century, Ellis Island was the chief point of entry for the millions of immigrants from Europe to the United States of America. For many years its reception halls lay empty, causing the immigrant poet, Eleni Mylonas, to observe,

> 'Disturbed by the sound of pigeon's wing, I heard voices of millions of people who came through here, building a temple with their highest joys and deepest sorrows – men and women who made it through to a new life, or who died straining to look through a dirty mirror at what they knew they could not possess.'

Today Ellis Island is a museum, and Mylonas' poetic description is only one of the many writings of former immigrants who had been chased across the Atlantic by the storm clouds of war, poverty, persecution, famine and ethnic cleansing. For me, one of the most moving reflections was from Katherine Beychok, a Russian Jewish immigrant who arrived at the gateway to new life in 1915, aged twelve. 'I saw this man coming towards me,' she wrote, 'and he was very beautiful. I didn't know he was my father . . . Later on I realized why he looked so familiar to me. He looked exactly like I did. But that's when I met him for the first time. And I fell in love with him and he with me . . . '

The reflections of both Mylonas and Beychok speak of something of the 'yearning [which] is both the beginning and the ending of the story' of our search for God, for new life, and of God's search for us. Katherine Beychok's experience of meeting her father for the first time has resonances with many people's description of their encounter with God. Some moment of disclosure opens a window in the soul and the beauty of familiarity, love, compassion, forgiveness, transformation is glimpsed, and there is the beginning of intimacy, of relationship. In that disclosure too there lies the possibility of the look-alike.

When I began exploring Ignatian spirituality I was reflecting on the story of Moses and the burning bush. Ignatian spirituality makes great play on the two elements of Scripture and the imagination. I had re-read much of the story of Moses, from his miraculous delivery from the holocaust engulfing the Jewish slave workers in Goshen, through his enforced exile because of his murder of a sadistic overseer, to his marriage and call to return to liberate God's people in Egypt. I thought, too, of Jethro, his father-in-law, who had provided him with a refuge and a role model. On the mountain in the wilderness Moses had time to reflect on his life, the plight of his people, his own act of betrayal, and his relative safety.[8]

In the privacy of a retreat house bedroom I enacted the story in which Moses sees the burning bush.[9] Earlier, it had been suggested I prayed the simple words, 'Lord, reveal to me the Father.' Moses did not know his father, though of course God did, and in the 'voice' that Moses heard, God acknowledges this: 'I am the God of your ancestors, the God of Abraham' – the father who would have killed the one he most loved, if it had not been for God;[10] 'the God of Isaac', the husband of Rebekah, the father of Jacob, whose name means 'deceiver' and 'wrestler', the one with whom God nearly lost the battle.[11] It occurred to me during this reflection that the God who reveals himself does so as the God of the unknown father; of a paranoid, Abraham; a wimp, Isaac; and Jacob, a deceiver and a wrestler who nearly defeats God.

For a few moments I was overcome by the profundity of the revelation: if God was portraying himself to Moses as the father, not of the saint, but of the paranoid, the wimp, the deceiver, the one who must win at all costs, then this was the God who was revealing himself to me. I remember taking off my shoes as part of my enactment of the story. Two truths were revealed: the first, regardless of background, parentage, flawed personality, failure or success, the need to win, I was both bad enough and good enough to be loved. Second, the insistence by God that Moses should feel the earth as holy, was to understand a God who identifies with the poorest, those with no shoes. It was as if God were saying, 'Bare feet are good enough for the poor to stand before me. What makes you so special?'

When Moses received this revelation, it is said that he 'covered his face, for he was afraid to look at God.' For a few moments I too understood that fear. Some years before I had spent time travelling in Latin America visiting groups and communities among priests and religious who had made what the Medellin Conference of Catholic Bishops had called the 'gospel option for the poor'. For the first time I was beginning to comprehend what this 'option' was: the very option that God himself made for his people in captivity; to Moses in his captivity to his illegitimacy, his enforced compromise with the oppressors of God's people, and his real fear at the consequences of his discernment of who God *really* is.

GROWING UP TO MATURITY

Within the Christian spiritual tradition lies the notion that we are to be imitators, mirror images of God. Moreover, the God whom we meet 'has not given us a spirit of fear, but of power, and of love, and of a sound mind.'[12] The God whom we meet as God seeks our wholeness, our salvation – our *salus* (the Latin word for healing, salvation). And the purpose of our encounters is not that we should remain in our childishness but, as St Paul puts it, 'that we should grow up to the full stature of our humanity in Jesus Christ.'[13]

Jesus puts the mystery of intimacy with God like this: 'You

must therefore be perfect, just as your heavenly Father is perfect.'[14] This text always puzzled and somewhat unnerved me, until one day I gave it some attention to try to get underneath its somewhat austere nature. After some struggling, I found myself jotting down a translation which seemed to me to cover both its richness and hope as a statement: 'Become whole, a completely integrated, uncontradictory person, having the same integrity as your Father in heaven.'

It is this sense of integrity that intuitively the child in us seeks from God. Integrity, that most demanding of virtues, contains within it the capacity to 'know the truth about ourselves making us humble and open to the truth in the world.'[15] Much of the distortion of our image of God as loving parent has been due to the influence of St Augustine. Augustine's father was an abusive parent, who regularly beat his son under the misapprehension that such discipline was necessary to beat evil and evil desires out of him. His mother often watched such thrashings and laughed at the misfortunes of her son. Augustine prayed that he would be delivered from punishment, and he was later to reflect that God's failure to deliver him led him subsequently to believe that God, too, wished for evil to be disciplined out of people.

It is possible for a child to experience incredible hardship without seeing it as punishment, and to grow from that to a place of wonder and worship. Gene Beerens, who worked for many years in inner-city Grand Rapids on the shores of Lake Michigan with prisoners on licence, tells the story of a black woman, a migrant worker in her seventies, in a Bible study group discussing the saying of Jesus, 'You are the salt of the earth.' Gene asked, 'What does it mean to be the salt of the earth?' The woman replied by telling the group how when she was a child her parents were poor sharecroppers, migrant workers who followed the harvests across the states each summer. Money was short and there was only one meal a day. Every morning from the age of eight, she and her sister would go into the fields with only a block of salt for nourishment. The salt was to prevent dehydration from the hot sun. 'To us,' said the woman, 'salt was a matter of life and death. We're the ones who prevent the world from dehydrating.'

Such an insight is not only profound, but once again exposes how the child in us perceives truth and, as Elisabeth O'Connor says, 'opens us to truth in the world.' The naturalist and oceanographer, Barry Lopez, recalls,

> the most moving look I ever saw from a child in the woods was on a mud bar by the footprints of a heron. We were on our knees, making handprints beside the footprints. You could feel the creek vibrating in the silt and sand. The sun beat down heavily on our hair. Our shoes were soaking wet. The look said, "I did not know until now that I would need someone much older to confirm this, the feeling I have of life here. I can now grow older, knowing it need never be lost."

Lopez comments that as the child discovers truth, beauty and him or herself, the right of the adult to impose on that discovery is very, very limited. 'If one speaks, it should only be to say, as well as one can, how wonderfully all this fits together, to indicate what a long, fierce peace can derive from the knowledge.'[16]

Such experience one longs for all children: to enjoy innocence, wonder and discovery in peace, and if not prosperity, then certainly security and safety. For most of the world's children such well-being is what Marcel Möring has called a 'great longing'. He records a conversation between a family of bereaved children:

> 'You know what's gone, don't you?'
>
> 'Papa, Mama,' she said, 'and God, and the mystery of love.' Her eyes filled.
>
> 'All that's left is memory,' she said, 'and the memory's not enough, the memory's one great longing.'[17]

The 'great longing' for me has something to do with our distortion of who God is. If, at some level, Moses 'covered his face for he was afraid to look at God', because he could not bear the truth about God as liberator, as one who took sides, who refused to be spiritualized, then anything less in our understanding of God creates an emptiness, and with it a longing to find the truth.

CHILDREN CANNOT BE MARTYRS

On the slopes of Slieve League in Donegal, Ireland, there are the ruins of a famine cottage. We occasionally stay in a refurbished modernized cottage next door. During the nineteenth century the potato crop, the staple food of peasant communities, failed, causing famine. Amid the desperate hardship, landlords torched the thatched roofs of the cottages of those unable to pay their rents, driving families into starvation or emigration – sometimes both. Donegal is a heartachingly beautiful place; as one native said, 'God was in good form the day he made it.' We go to Donegal for the tranquillity, the isolation and the splendour, to recharge batteries of worn-out life. But it was once a thriving landscape where communities of people made their livelihoods, their homes and their dreams.

John M. Feehan bids the modern visitor to these wild parts to

> sit down outside the door [of one of the famine cottage ruins] and transport yourself back a hundred years. Imagine that it was you who built this little house, stone by stone, plank by plank; that you brought your beautiful young bride here full of the joy of boundless love; that you began married life here, brought children into the world, paid your rent and worked twelve or fourteen hours a day just to rear your family and barely keep them alive; then one day you and your family are evicted, the home you built is crowbarred to the ground. Hear the cries and lamentations of your wife and children – your children – and perhaps you may get some idea of the horror and savagery of it all.[18]

I have sat there on several evenings, and on the doorsteps of children suffering from famine in Africa. One day in Malawi I arrived at Matope, a town whose name translates as 'mud'. That day it was hard-baked earth, the stream that gave its 'muddiness' had long since dried up. Children scoured long empty bowls for the faintest scrapings of mealie flour. The priest, Martin Mgeni, explained how the price of the flour had risen four-fold. His family of ten children suffered from malnutrition. In a piece I wrote for *The Guardian* I reflected that the 'price of food was loyalty to the government. Parish clergy spoke of the inequitable distribution of maize in government handouts, revealing that the most needy are "simply not entitled . . ." '[19] I went on to comment about threats and coercion, and that the true victims were the innocents, the children.

Such experiences raise questions over the optimism, not only of contemporary Western society, but even the psalmist who records, 'I have not seen the righteous forsaken, nor his children begging bread.'[20] I have seen forsakenness and begging. I have seen 'the tongue of the baby at the breast stick to its palate for thirst; little children ask for bread [but] no one gives them any.'[21] Martin Mgeni was certainly righteous, if sharing the little he had with those who had even less is a mark of righteousness. God speaks through the psalmist of his vocation, 'I will satisfy the poor with bread.'[22] But throughout the history of God's dealing with people, the way in which God provides is through people of justice, who understand that compassion is the very essence of true godliness.

The child can only be victim in such circumstances. Emil Fackenheim observed that 'children cannot be martyrs'. He was speaking in the aftermath of Auschwitz, of course, but his insight is universal. 'There is about martyrdom an element of choice. To be victim in the way the Auschwitz children were victim is an incomprehensible horror.'

WHY SOME PEOPLE CARE . . . WHY SO FEW?

What is so disturbing to the soul is the degree to which, even with the evidence in front of one's eyes and not filtered through the television screen, the ease with which one settles back into apathy is truly shocking. Elie Wiesel tells of a meeting of Righteous Gentiles in New York who were called together to find out why some people care, and, why so few? Wiesel says, 'Most who cared were simple people who didn't even know that what they were doing was courageous; they didn't even know it was heroic . . . They did it because it was the thing to do. And I felt woe to our society if to be human becomes an heroic act.'[23] Yet increasingly this is so in terms of the children, the little ones of our world.

Paradoxically, however, the hope lies in the children. In 1987 I visited the Sojourners community in Washington, DC. One of the families was being assessed for the possibility of adopting a little black girl into their family. The social worker talking to the children asked the eldest son what he would want to do for his new little sister. 'I would tell her not to pick up syringes in the alley.' The social worker nearly wept. Jim Wallis, who told me this story, said, 'That is the essence of the gospel in this neighbour-hood: one without syringes, where people can have a safe backyard. But,' he continued, 'until the middle class enters into solidarity with the poor, nothing will change; the poor cannot do it by themselves. Much of the responsibility for social and gospel change lies with progressive white Christians. Unless we recognize our responsibility and quit saying we don't know what needs to be changed, then nothing will change.'

The *undersong* of the child whispers the 'great longing' for a new order, a new world that is both outer and inner – where there is integrity, wholeness, safety and justice. Two young girls, prisoners in Auschwitz, tell of their desire to keep the rituals of freedom.

> One night Edith and I talked about how we used to celebrate Sabbath at home. The kapos went back and forth during the night beating anybody who whispered, but Edith said, "Why don't we pray? Why don't we pretend that we are at home and setting the table?" We would do this every Friday night and murmur the Sabbath prayer. It gave us some kind of normality in hell. One Friday we were standing by the latrine when Edith said, "It is almost Shabbat." I said, "Why don't we celebrate inside the latrine. They won't hear us there, we can sing." The SS never came to the latrine because it was so horrible.
>
> We stood in a corner away from the others, and we started to sing the songs sung every Friday in every Jewish home. And as we sang other children from Germany, Hungary, and Czechoslovakia came around and started to sing with us.

> From then on, every Friday night we celebrated the Sabbath in the latrine at Auschwitz.[24]

Against the background of such stories there is a rightful silence, a sort of speechlessness, a refusal to allow for the slick word or the easy response. Such stories put into perspective our own petty differences, our saccharine-sweet individualistic faith and its attendant escapism. The Hebrew concept of the world is a house or household. It is both the creation and the dwelling place of God. John, the author of the Apocalypse, sees the vision of a Holy City as the hope and utopia for all humanity: 'Look, here God lives among human beings. He will make *his home among them; they will be his people*, and he will be their God, *God-with-them*.'[25] The *undersong* of the child within cries out for a restoration of that household. For, as Daniel Romero has observed, 'The house of God should be a safe and secure place for all God's children, not as an escape, but as a place where people are free to be who they are without pretence.'[26]

What children like Alice Lok Cahana and her friend Edith discovered in Auschwitz is eloquently put by Richard Rohr,

> To pray is to build your own house. To pray is to discover that someone else is within your house. To pray is to recognise that it is not your house at all. To keep praying is to have no house to protect because there is only one House. And that One House is everybody's Home. That is the politics of prayer. And that is probably why truly spiritual people are always a threat to politicians of any sort. They want our allegiance and we can no longer give it. Our House is too big.[27]

This is the missing dimension of the 'mystery of love', which only the child bereft of the True Parent can understand and long for.

When we allow the *undersong* of the child within us to be heard, we find that we have to address somewhere deep within us the questions, 'Where are you?' 'What are you doing here?' 'Who are you looking for?' For each of us the answers will be different in the detail, but at some level they will return to the longing of the taxi driver – to know that we are loved.

2

THE UNDERSONG OF CONVERSION

I WAS WALKING THROUGH ONE OF São Paolo's many *favelas* with an old friend, Pat. We passed one of the hundreds of shacks that are home to many of Brazil's landless and dispossessed. A woman greeted us, and we had a short conversation. Later he told me her story, how she had come in from the country with nothing and had approached him to ask if he could help her find somewhere to live. He was sympathetic, but in the end had to leave the woman to help herself. Some days later he met her again. 'Come and see,' she said and led him into her 'home'. Inside, furniture was placed down the centre of the room and around the sides. 'This is where I live,' she said. Pat asked her why she didn't make more room by re-ordering the furniture. 'You don't understand,' she replied, 'you see the people who own this place, they live with their family and three children on that side of the room, and I live with my children on this side.' Pat mused to me, 'We preach the gospel – these folk live it.'

How we 'live the gospel' matters. But of course how we 'understand' the gospel determines how we subsequently 'live' it. Much of how we both understand and live it depends upon our place in the order of things. Someone who has known only poverty, rejection and a lack of worth will perceive the gospel very differently from someone who has enjoyed a certain degree of economic well-being, security and affection, and some sense of certainty about themselves.

Some prostitutes regularly gathered around the edge of a large cathedral in Latin America. They would never venture into the sanctuary or even into the nave with the congregation. Alfredo, the French priest, asked them to come in. 'No,' they replied, 'we are too sinful.' Somehow they had internalized the sense of sinfulness associated with their prostitution. 'We do things that are unspeakable,' they said. One day the priest persuaded them to come to the sanctuary. 'Do you believe you are forgiven?' he asked them. 'No. We are too sinful.' 'Do you believe you have committed the worst sins?' 'Yes. We are the greatest sinners,' they concluded. 'God loves you the most,' said Alfredo, and told them the story of the woman who washed Jesus' feet with her hair. 'Now do you believe you are forgiven?' 'A little,' they replied. The priest called for a bucket of water and washed the feet of each of the women. Finally he asked, 'Do you believe you are forgiven now?' 'A lot more.' The priest took the bucket and poured the water over himself. 'I am the greatest sinner. But I am washed with the grace of the forgiveness of God's love. Now do you believe?' 'Yes,' they agreed.

I consciously became a Christian at the age of fourteen. One Guy Fawkes night I attended a service in the local church where the preacher was a 'converted' footballer. I wasn't that interested in football, but I had been sent to Sunday school and church for as much of my life as I could remember, and since we had just moved house again, church was the only place I really knew in the neighbourhood. I remember making my commitment to Jesus Christ, confessing that I was a sinner, and being told that I was now converted too. Being converted was quite important, because the kind of churches we attended were full of people who had been converted, and not to be among them was to be different.

When I look back on what happened it is easy to see the insecurities and lack of a sense of self-worth that were in some sense the background to my coming to faith. The gospel I was led to believe in was a highly individual and personal one, which guaranteed my salvation from sin and hell and ensured a place in heaven. The mission of this gospel was to win others to the same experience, and to live a good life. I did this faithfully for many years, and in no way do I want to dismiss the experience: it was undoubtedly for me, at the time, the way in which God took hold of my life. Guilt and sin were still quite big things in the late 1950s, particularly over sex and the like. My frequent moves with my itinerant parents meant that I never felt I really had any roots, and I was constantly having to make new friends. Girls were a fascination, but the chat-up lines rarely worked! I developed quite a line in 'story-telling' – lying to you and me! This frequently got me into trouble, because I was usually found out. I remember the night I made my commitment going straight to the office of one of my youth leaders and telling him about it, in part because he was the greatest exposer of my stories!

Much of my early life was lived within a primarily white, middle-class, Protestant community. My parents were deeply suspicious of Roman Catholics, and around our house from time to time would be almost fundamentalist polemical pamphlets and books against popery and Romish practices. My mother had come from C.T. Russell's 'International Bible Students', a sect which eventually became the Jehovah's Witnesses. As a trainee pharmacist she had become an Anglican, though she flirted with Baptists and other nonconformists along the way.

CONVERSATION AND CONVERSION

For me the passing years have changed my thinking on the nature of conversion, though I am convinced that the human spirit both needs and requires change, and that it is an infinitely longer and more adventurous process than that which is transacted in a distinct moment. With Orlando Costas, I see it as both the 'distinct moment and a continuous process'. And it is the *undersong* of that process, that living and practice of the gospel, that becomes the imperative of spiritual life.

As with most words, it is often good to go back to the roots to discover their meaning. Ched Myers, who has done so much valuable work on the Scriptures, particularly the Gospel of St Mark, observed in an article in *Sojourners*, 'We need the discipline of conversation (from the Middle English *conversen*, meaning *to associate with)*; also from the Latin (*conversus* meaning *to turn around*). Conversation holds within it the possibility of mutual conversion.'[1]

In the world in which we live, where all too many are like the woman and her family in the *favela*, it takes some believing to say, as Thomas Merton did,

> It is a glorious destiny to be a member of the human race, though it is a race dedicated to many absurdities, and one which may make terrible mistakes, yet with all that, God gloried in becoming a member of the human race! . . . There is no way of telling people that they are walking around shining like the sun . . . There are no strangers! If only we could see each other (as we really are) all the time, there would be no more war, no more hatred, no more anxiety; no more greed . . . I suppose the big problem would be that we would fall down and worship each other . . . The gate of heaven is everywhere.[2]

Yet Merton is right, the vision of God for the human race still lies in the dream of Genesis, 'God created man in the image of himself, in the image of God he created him, male and female he created them.' Then the divine accolade, 'God saw all he had made, and indeed it was very good.'[3] The problem lies in getting there, in our ability to *turn around* and our capacity *to associate with* those who because of their perceived difference from us both prevent, and potentially enable, our *conversus.*

It is our perception of opposites that so often prevents the development of our 'glorious destiny' to be fully human. The African feminist theologian, Khumo Nthlag, reflects that

> Christ reconciles life's opposites, rich and poor, master and servant, black and white, rich and poor, male and female. In uniting the basic pair of opposites, male and female, in his own person living out the consequences of that fully integrated personality, Jesus has not only shown us the way, but has enabled us to integrate all the opposites that conspire to pull us apart, through his Spirit in us.[4]

To embrace such a vision calls for a change of view, of loyalty, even of gods, if necessary. Jürgen Moltmann raises a rhetorical question, 'Does modern society have a future? Its future is repentance.' The root meaning of repentance is 'to look for a better way'.[5]

I was visiting a primary school one morning. The head teacher told me that she had been teaching the children about repentance. 'One side of the assembly hall is called "sin",' she said, 'the other is "life".' Turning to the children she asked, 'How do you get from "sin" to "life"?' Quick as a flash an eight-year-old girl raised her hand and said, 'You run as fast you can!' The little girl was paralysed; her legs were in callipers, she would never walk, let alone run. There is a parable here, for conversion does require a moving from one side to the other, and various things paralyse – indifference, addiction to other, perhaps more attractive options; or more sinisterly, prejudice, class, economic circumstances, or just plain old-fashioned hardness of heart!

The rich young man in his encounter with Jesus did not find it possible to make the journey from where he was to 'life'. The demand of Jesus that he 'sell possessions and give the money to the poor', did not seem to the rich man to be worthwhile. Whereas Peter, who went to find Jesus too, 'left everything and followed'.[6] Getting to the place where the 'reconciliation of life's opposites' becomes possible depends a great deal on the starting point.

STARTING WITH THE REALITIES AS WE KNOW THEM

There is a sense that we start on the journey of conversion with the realities as we know them – experience as it is lived. Some years ago a guest came to stay in our house. From the moment the taxi drew up at the door and the person emerged, I sensed something was not quite as it seemed. I opened the door to a tall blond German who stepped over the threshold and dropped a couple of bags to the floor. 'I have come for change,' the strong German accent declared. Showing the guest to the room, I called my wife on the phone, 'I think you'd better come home,' I said, 'to meet our guest – now!' We were used to people coming for a sight-seeing visit to London, but this person was here for another reason, which soon became apparent – the last treatment for a sex change operation, completing the transformation into 'Maria'.

Things did not go simply. Maria (not her real name) was obsessed with 'herself'. The money did not arrive for her operation and she quickly ran out. She was anxious. My wife Dee ended up doing all the negotiations on the telephone with the hospital. By the end of the week she owed us more money than we had been paid by the agency!

For the first couple of days we felt angry, cheated out of our normal happy-go-lucky holidaying guests; we wanted 'Maria' to leave! As the days passed, and 'Maria' became more open, we found ourselves touched by the vulnerability of it all, as well as the sadness. I do not know whether we were seeing 'Maria' as she really was. Yet at the same time we grew to admire the struggle, determination to become something different, and the true cost. The situation judged us: either we had to change, or move into isolationism and hostility – simple as that.

As we reflected on this experience, we began to recognize it as a gift. We talked it over with a friend who observed, 'There is no logic to this gift except the logic that is gift. Gratuitousness is what redeems the world; they go to find, they give to receive. Gift is connected with simplicity, originality and weakness.' Our weakness, in the form of prejudice, had been challenged; so had our sense of hospitality – how easy to give it to those who cause us no anxiety, raise no questions, take acceptance as a matter of course. It is often in the uncomfortable, the unexpected, that the revelation of God is to be experienced, and transformation becomes possible. There was a 'gate of heaven' experience, as Merton would put it. I think it was Meister Eckhart who reflected, 'Everything we need to be co-creators of a world that is one, is already available to us. We need only the courage to plumb our depths to discover our indwelling God, in whom all is one.'

A PEOPLE MAKING THEIR OWN HISTORY

Part of the dilemma for contemporary Christianity is that it has become embroiled in internal struggles that threaten to overwhelm it. In addition, the language it uses to communicate its message has lost much of its power, because the words have become empty and without content. The early Christian communities knew what they were up against; all the words in their vocabulary were in the vocabulary of the powerful. Pablo Richard has shown us that

> within the Roman Empire the term "salvation" (*soteria*) is political; it designates the peace, security and welfare the empire provides. The martyrs recognise that salvation comes from God and the Lamb. They are in effect saying that it does not come from the Roman Emperor and his empire, nor is it individual salvation affecting the soul: it is social and bodily, although the personal and spiritual are not excluded.[7]

Other words such as 'force' (*dynamis*) and 'reign' (*basilea*) and 'power' (*exousia*) 'are political terms and take their inspiration from Psalm 2.'

For those of us living in the West, in Europe or the United States, the 'salvation' offered by the State is very considerable. Most contemporary Christianity relies upon an unwritten constitution of uncritical alliance with the political, economic and military hegemony that controls Western materialism and its predominance in the international market-place. And sensitivities are very tender. One of the most demanding questions I have ever had to face was put to me by Jim Wallis: 'Where do you place your security?' he asked. My reflection led me to realize that who God was in the process of security came a long way down the list, after money, my social status, the security of the nuclear shield, and my place in a democracy.

The late Robert Runcie, as Archbishop of Canterbury, used his sermon at the Falklands War Thanksgiving Service to critique 'gung-ho' attitudes to war from those who stayed well away, and he experienced the full wrath of the leader of the government of the day, the tabloid press and much else besides. *Faith in the City*, a report Runcie commissioned to look at poverty and deprivation in inner cities and outer estates, came in for similar panning as a 'Marxist manifesto'. It wasn't, of course, but for a few fleeting moments it seemed as if gospel values were the subject of the

Church's concern, and its language and message found a hearing. For a little while it seemed as if the fear of relegation to a footnote of history had been overcome by the daring possibility that we might rewrite our history as the people of God.

Such moments are fleeting, but it was as if something had been touched and a new conversion was possible. Joan Chittister, a Benedictine sister, has observed of the *undersong* of conversion, that

> We need a new image of God.
> We need a new respect for the poor and exploited.
> We need a new model of woman.
> We need a new kind of man.
> We need new models of holy madness,
>   and wisdom, and justice and fire.
> We need a new kind of conscience, and a new sense
>   of God's righteous anger.
> We need a commitment to non-force
>   and a sense of gentle strength.
> We need exemplars of all these things
>   or how shall we ever come to them in ourselves,
>   in our time, at our age, with our greatest needs.[8]

At an exhibition of the decline of the Inuit people of the Arctic, one of the museum notes, written by Robert André, declared: 'We must again become a people making our own history. To be able to make our own history is to be able to mould our own future, to build a society that preserves the best of our past traditions, while enabling us to go on and develop as a whole people.'[9] This, too, is a parable for Christian people and the Church in our time. Where people through oppression, poverty or exile have been forced to make their own history, new energies have emerged in theologies of liberation, of life, of women, of black people and so on. There has been a rediscovery of language and its meaning. It has regained a power and influence that offers a hope for the hopeless, and radical critique for the powerful.

My experience of churches, particularly of the evangelical tradition, is that they rely on certain 'trigger' words such as 'salvation', 'reign (of God)', and 'power', as well as 'repentance 'and 'forgiveness' to be part of the stock phrases of sermons. But if such words are to have any real meaning in our time, then history-making requires a fresh understanding of what it means to be the new people of God. The essential energy for an effective understanding of the *undersong* of conversion is love. Increasingly I have discovered that such love has what might be described as a political content, insofar as it draws us into reflection and action on behalf of the most vulnerable, as well as desiring for them, as for all others, that God is known and loved.

POOR AS ICON OF CHRIST

Catherine de Hueck Doherty was the founder of Madonna House in New York for the hungry poor. Her roots were in the Russian aristocracy, and she married into a wealthy family. She became dissatisfied with the trivia that seemed so integral to the lifestyle of the idle rich and decided after something of a dramatic conversion to dedicate her life to the poor, whom she was to describe as the 'icon of Christ'. What touched her most were the face-to-face encounters that she had with those whom many regarded as the off-scourings of society.

'The hunger for God,' she wrote, 'can only be satisfied by a love that is face to face, person to person. It is only in the eyes of another that we can find the icon of Christ. We must make the other person aware that we love them. If we do, they will know that God loves them. They will never hunger again.'[10]

A couple of years ago I was asked to lead some Bible studies on the Gospel of Mark in the parish of St John Waterloo, in London. Every night on the portico of this famous church many of London's homeless sleep. Whenever I enter the church I have a conversation with the folks, and on a particularly cold night, one of the regulars said to me, 'I hope Jesus comes tonight . . . '

Once inside, we reflected on that encounter. 'What,' I questioned, 'would it mean for Jesus to come tonight for those on the church steps?' I should of course have added, 'And for us?' As we reflected, people responded: a roof over their heads, proper food, clothing, cleanliness, acceptance, belonging – embrace, unconditional friendship. I found myself asking, 'And us?' Of course the words of the Gospel of Matthew came rushing at me: 'When did we see you hungry and feed you?' And the King will reply, 'Inasmuch as you fed the least important, you fed me.'[11]

Conversion is a process of turning around and associating with those whom we meet both as we turn, and because we turn. When I consciously began my faith journey, what was important to me was making a spirituality that saw the church as an 'ark of salvation', and the company of its people my exclusive companions, save for those who, through witness to my and others' testimony of personal salvation, joined it too. Such a world view led me into a narrow extremism that in the end became spiritually disabling. I found myself constantly not coming up to the mark of others whom I perceived as living better lives than me; but equally I became frustrated with the lack of realism, and perhaps even more, the lack of compassion, even élitism which marked the spirit within the 'ark'.

No particular moment marked the 'turning point', or the 'looking for a better way', but a number of circumstances combined to open my faith up to new possibilities. Among these was meeting and subsequently marrying a woman from Northern Ireland. Shortly after our marriage the euphemistically named 'Troubles' broke out, and the thirty-year war of violence and mayhem began. Not in our marriage, I hasten to add! Walking the burning streets of Belfast one night late in 1969 with a Christian minister whose parish it was, we found ourselves knocking on the doors of boarded-up houses condemned by the local housing authority. Inside were refugees, families whose homes on the nearby mixed Catholic and Protestant housing estates had been burned down. We talked to them and shared their ordeal as they described how armed men had forced them to leave, and how their neighbours had cried as they stood by, helplessly watching the burnings. At that moment there was no bitterness towards those who had been their neighbours; there was confusion, regret, anger, and a feeling of powerlessness and futility towards the perpetrators of violence.

CREATIVE DISLOCATION

For me at that moment the men of violence were there to be angry with, and to hate. My 'closed system' thinking told me that sin had led them into hatred and violence. It shut the book. It was simple: they were sinners. I did not have to think about the sense of injustice, the overwhelming frustration of powerlessness; the pain of unemployment, of inadequate housing; the feeling of being manipulated – all contributing to the meaninglessness that caused the sin, expressed through violence, to emerge. What I recognized in that early encounter was something that is integral to true conversion, what Robert McAfee-Brown describes as 'creative dislocation'. Such 'creative dislocation' motivates the individual to go 'to the oppressed, stand with them, see the world from their view point, and figure out what God is saying to you.'[12] This process of 'seeing the world from their view point' is integral to the 'conversation that leads to mutual conversion.' But it is not a dialogue or conversation that is held in a vacuum, nor in the absence of God. John Robinson, in his sermon to the pilgrims boarding the *Mayflower* in 1620, advised his hearers, 'I urge you to study the gospels. When you think you have the answer, go back and read some more. You'll find you don't have the answer. It is something perpetually elusive, and you must always search for it.'

Reading the gospel is a matter of perspective. So too is interpretation. That is not to say there is no objectivity to gospel truth, or hearing God's word today; there is, but we read the Bible from the space we occupy. When we move into a different space, and begin to observe the text from an upside-down point of view, we need to find tools to interpret it. Some years ago Walter Wink, who has done considerable work on the Gospel texts in relation to our understanding of the Kingdom of God, once had me strip to my underwear on stage at a conference on mission! It was all in a good cause. We were exploring the passage in Luke's Gospel where Jesus is telling his followers how to behave in the new order: 'To anyone who slaps you on the right cheek, present the other as well,' says Jesus.[13]

Traditionally we have seen this text as a sort of 'eat dirt' instruction. There are two ways of hitting someone on the right cheek; one is with the left hand – but in the Middle East no one touches another with the left hand because it is associated with cleaning after toilet – so the other way of hitting is with the back of the right hand. Such a gesture is dismissive and demeaning. Jesus, while not inviting the Christian to retaliate, nevertheless suggests a gesture that comes close to the risk of retaliation. 'Offer the other cheek,' he advises. This means that the assailant is being offered the risk of a fight, but also the demand from his potential victim that he, or she, be treated as an equal.

We acted out the text that led to my clerical striptease! It was the injunction by Jesus, 'If someone wishes to take your cloak from you, do not refuse your tunic.' In a court of law a judge could require a debtor without money to give up his cloak as surety against the debt. Such a person would be very poor indeed and, to make a point, Jesus argues that the insistence on the surety of the cloak by the one to whom the debt is owed, should be exposed for its meanness and inhumanity. Giving up, in addition, the tunic, or the undergarment, would expose the unfortunate individual to nakedness. In most societies shame on seeing the nakedness of another falls on the witness, not on the one who is naked. Occasionally in times of oppression women in different cultures have used this weapon of non-violence to protest against their oppressors and to shame them.

Looking at texts like these in this way, and indeed revisiting much of the Gospel narrative from the perspective of the underside, not only converts one's outlook, but gives a whole new impetus to both the nature, content and the intention of the Christian message. Seeing Jesus as one who non-violently confronted injustice, and who commended in his hearers daily acts of resistance against injustice, offers fresh inspiration and hope for the creation of *peace on earth* that the angelic messengers foretold at his birth. What this process of hearing God's word for today requires is not only a consideration of the *text* – the Bible – but also of what is going on around it in the community, or *context* from which the *text* is read. And all of this depends on an awareness of the real-life situations of the readers and hearers, the *pre-text* from which the gospel is read. This sometimes means that we have to discover that 'what for us is upside down is right side up for other people'.[14]

My own journey into 'creative dislocation', of standing with people whose world view is different from my own, has opened up the possibility of a gospel that sees salvation not only in terms of personal forgiveness, peace of mind and well-being, but also in terms of social harmony, peacemaking and the curtailment of conflict through keeping and going beyond the law of love.

FORGIVENESS – WHATEVER

New understanding of forgiveness has been an integral element of this dislocation, or re-location. In a sense, too, it is central to the 'looking for a better way', not least because what I have always understood about forgiveness remains. 'Know thyself and be at peace with the world,' remarked the nineteenth-century French poet, Charles Péguy. More than most I need the daily grace of God for forgiveness in my life, from the pettiness that so often mars relationships, to the heavier sins of unresolved anger; as well as the resistance to moving from loyalty to my class, culture and environment towards those without privilege, power and influence.

I have witnessed the act of forgiveness among people in great danger, and I have heard their stories, which have profoundly moved and humbled me. During a visit to El Salvador in the 'dirty war' of the 1980s, I was visiting a remote village with a group of Americans and Australians. To reach this community required a long bus ride, then a march through the jungle. We came upon a clearing where several dozen families eked out a living on the side of a mountain. They welcomed us with open arms. Within a short while we were sitting down to a meal of chicken and rice and beans, the ubiquitous Coca Cola, and fresh fruit. The feast was little short of a miracle. All supplies for the village required the long trek we had made, except for vegetables and fruit. Two days before our arrival, government forces had arrived by helicopter paranoid in their search for FMLN guerillas. They had discovered the villagers' food store, and on the pretext that 'you must be hiding *banditos*' had removed in several flights all the villagers' foodstuffs. As we talked, what became evident was the lack of bitterness, of anger. Neither did there seem to be resentment: it was as if they understood the plight of their oppressors.

A day or so later we trekked up country to visit a group of guerillas in the mountains. The journey was arduous and not a little dangerous. As we approached a clearing, a small number of men and women emerged from the woods. Our discussions were friendly and there was real concern in their questions. 'When we achieve power,' they asked us, 'how should we behave towards our enemies?' We discussed with them the issue of forgiveness, illustrating it from the experience of priests such as Ernesto Cardenal in Nicaragua and others who found ways of dealing with their former enemies. There was genuine willingness to see forgiveness as a political option, and their response was thoughtful.

On another occasion a group of El Salvadorean refugees were forced to flee their village following military action. After several days they took stock and made time for confession. What did they confess? One said, 'I didn't want to bury the dead. It becomes an act of mercy just to bury our dead.' Another confessed, 'Some of us had a little bread and others did not. Many people hid their bread even though they saw other people going hungry.' The group continued to recall the selfish things they had done, and asked God's forgiveness, singing, 'Lord, have mercy on your people.'

While I was at Maryknoll in New York, the home of the Catholic Missionary Society of America, a friend told me of the visit of Jon Sobrino, a survivor of the massacre of six Jesuit priests and two Salvadorean workers on 16 November 1989. Sobrino had been absent when his colleagues and their two support workers were killed by military assassins. Those who had gathered to hear Sobrino expected him to attack American imperialism and its involvement in El Salvador. Instead, he spoke on the covenant and forgiveness. He illustrated his theme with the powerful story of an El Salvadorean woman whose sons had been killed and daughter gang-raped, who spoke of her forgiveness of the perpetrators. Of another he reported that when challenged by her priest to forgive she had responded, 'Father, I will try.' His listeners grew restless, and expressed irritation. They had come for a political ear pounding, but Sobrino had to remind them that nothing more nor less than forgiveness would bring the healing that El Salvador needed, and a fresh covenant between all sides and God.

Such stories provide something of those exemplars that Joan Chittister indicated were necessary if we are to find 'new images of God, new models of women, new kinds of men, new models of holy madness, and a new conscience, non force, and a sense of gentle strength.'

My experience of 'creative dislocation' in El Salvador and many other places has opened up for me something of the need to be converted from the arrogance of 'top down' or imperial theology towards one that is marked by the power to liberate, making reconciliation and deep forgiveness possible within the psyche of humanity. Part of this has to do with how we perceive not only the task of salvation, but also the role of the self, and the transforming process. What constantly surprises me in the stories of human beings in their struggles against the powers and principalities, whether in El Salvador or elsewhere, is the almost total absence of egotism – whereas Western Christianity is obsessed with what Bill Burrows has called 'self interested clinging', and the 'strengthening of the anxious ego and the self deception of ego'.[15] Such obsession leads to the perception that salvation is about the meeting, or assuaging of human needs, rather than 'a surrendering to God who offers empowerment for a frighteningly new, self–transcending way of being in the world.'[16]

Shortly after my bypass operation in 1993 I went for a retreat. 'What is your heart's desire?' asked my spiritual director. 'What would it be like to be loved apart from the doing? If you couldn't do any more, what would the love of God mean to you then?' It was an invitation to re-invent my history in the name of Love. I cannot pretend that the retreat was easy, or that I came up with any lasting answer to the questions put to me. Too often, then and since, the text from Isaiah which has spoken to me has been true:

'Your salvation lay in conversion and tranquillity, your strength in serenity and trust, and you would have none of it.'[17]

At that time I was reading Rian Malan's book, *My Traitor's Heart*. It includes the account of a young white man in South Africa, Neil Alcock, who together with his wife chose to make his home among black South Africans. It was a radical step, and one that constantly faced them with threats from both white and black communities. They had entered this situation out of a desire to express solidarity and love. After Neil's violent death, Malan records how his widow sought to continue the vision, and commented, 'She believed in love, you see; not in a sentimental sense, nor a religious sense, but just . . . love: giving of yourself and trying to do good for others.'[18]

THIS IS THE WAY OF LOVE

My spiritual director Christine's questions had caused me to reflect on my 'broken heart' and the places in my own story where my heart had been 'broken' through failure, unrequited dreams, the struggle with institutional religion, and my own poor track record in personal relationships. Like the Alcocks, I 'believed in love', and I felt, too, that I had given my life in the service of God because of love. What I couldn't discern then was whether I could accept being loved apart from being a reward for 'doing'. What I knew at the time was that I was wounded: wounded physically with the scars of the operation, and wounded psychologically and spiritually because of the sense of futility of so much hard work.

I am one of those fortunate people who have always had a sense of the presence of God within and around me. I know Real Presence. Conversation with God is essentially intimate and, barring the absence or non-existence of God, it is real. During the early reflections of my time away then, I sensed God saying, 'You are wounded too because you share my dream; it too is a catalogue of heartbreak. So little of it has come to fulfilment.'

Discovering oneself loved is perhaps the most difficult aspect of the *undersong* of conversion. Part of that difficulty lies of course in understanding what love is, and what it is not. I found the Alcocks' insights helpful in understanding something of what

I felt back in 1993. They had experienced almost total misunder-standing of their vision, a sense of betrayal by those they thought they could trust, poverty, sickness, and ultimately death. At one particularly low point Neil Alcock reflected,

> 'I feel utterly betrayed by loving. All the things I'd ever been told about love just weren't true. It was all full of false promises. I understood that love was a safety and a protec-tion, and that if you loved you would be rewarded by someone loving you back, or at least not wanting to damage you. But it wasn't true, any of it. I knew that if I stayed, this was how it was going to be: it would never get any better; it would stay the same, or get worse.'

Later, he concluded, 'This is the way of love; down this road: look at it hard. This is where it is going to lead you.'

Neil Alcock's experience provides a sobering insight into the true cost of loving. Perhaps any invitation to accept the love of Christ should carry a health warning, for it seems to me that the experience of the Alcocks was more reflective of the kind of love that Jesus had in mind, when he spoke of being willing to lay down life, than the 'self interested clinging' that passes for loving in the Christian community today.

When I became a Christian, the emphasis upon the cross was much greater than I sense it is today. Certainly I believed that in some way, which I still struggle to understand, Christ died for me. What I understood somewhat better was that to follow Christ meant choosing a path of suffering, *taking up the cross*, as Jesus put it.[19] Reflecting on the Alcocks' sense of betrayal of their loving solidarity, I glimpsed a moment of insight into both the experience of Jesus, and myself. The cry from the cross, 'My God, my God, why have you forsaken me?' perhaps contained something of that despair articulated by the Alcocks' experience.

The issue of the cross in the *undersong* of conversion is critical to our understanding of the vocation of being Christian. Yet here I fall back on the words of the Pilgrim Father, John Robinson, quoted earlier in his urging to study the Gospels: 'When you think you have the answer, go back and read some more. You'll find you don't have the answer. It is something perpetually elusive, and you must always search for it.' I certainly think this is true of our understanding of the cross. During a visit to Nicaragua during the Sandinista era, one of the priests in the government at the time, Father Miguel d'Escoto, observed: 'I don't think we Christians have understood what carrying the cross means: the path of baptism. We are not carrying the cross when we are poor or sick, or suffering small everyday things. They are all part of life. The cross comes when we try to change things. That is how it came for Jesus.'

At the time I found this observation quite liberating. I had long since concluded that Jesus went to the cross not so much as a result of a divine edict, but more as a consequence of obedience to a vision. As he faced the demands and challenges of political, social and economic forces around him and challenged their legitimacy, so he became increasingly the focus for their anger and destructiveness. The end, juridical execution, was inevitable. But of course the cross is bigger than all of that. I wonder whether, if we really grasped the full implications of the choice of taking up the cross, would we in fact choose it?

It is impossible to observe the cross, however, without observing the undergirding energy of love that determines its possibility. However one views it – whether from the relatively matter-of-fact perspective of seeing it as a result of the choice by Jesus to be faithful to a vision for humanity to live in justice, love and peace; or whether the cross is a model of substitutional atonement – simply, one cannot get away from the driving energy of love.

LOVE TRANSCENDS DEFEAT

What is significant about the love that leads to and from the cross is that it is a love that is tested. Neil Alcock, like anyone under pressure facing the possibility of failure and even death, went through many stages in his quest to understand love. For me, the following observation comes closest to my understanding of the nature both of Christian discipleship and to a lesser extent an understanding of the cross:

'I think you know what I mean if I tell you love is worth
nothing until it has been tested by its own defeat. I felt I was
being asked to try to love enough not to be afraid of the
consequences. I realized that love, even when it ends in
defeat, gives you a kind of honour; but without love, you
have no honour at all. I think that is what I misunderstood
all my life. Love is to enable you to transcend defeat.'[20]

To choose the kind of loving that is 'not afraid of the consequences' requires a deep conviction that it must be worth it.
Our global village has reached a point in its history where
it cannot be neglected until we have sorted out the squabbling
over truth that so bedevils contemporary Christianity. The question that demands an answer is simply, 'What is it worth to follow
Jesus today?'

Conversion comes down to a fresh understanding of how God
sees things, and what in our times is good news. In John's Gospel
there is an account of the healing by Jesus of a blind man. The
prevailing cultural outlook of the time was that all deformity was
the consequence of sin, either in individuals themselves, or their
families. Jesus is asked: 'Rabbi, who sinned, this man or his
parents that he should have been born blind?' 'Neither he nor
his parents sinned,' Jesus answered, 'he was born blind so that the
works of God might be revealed in him.'[21] This story is pivotal in
the understanding of sin. Jesus turns the preconceptions held by
many, then and now, on their head. 'The revolution in the concept
of sin,' observes James Alison, 'consists in the following: at the
beginning of the tale, sin was considered in terms of some sort of
defect that excludes the one bearing the defect. At the end of the
tale, sin is considered as an act of exclusion: the real blindness is
the blindness which is not only present in those who exclude, but
actually grows and intensifies during the act of exclusion.'[22] Or, to
put it another way, 'Sin is not what excludes in the person of the
excluded one, but the dynamic act of excluding in the persons of
the excluders.'

More and more, my journey has led me into this understanding
of the nature of sin – that it is the act of excluding. A lovely story
I heard some years ago offers a further insight both into sin and

forgiveness. A tribe in the upper reaches of the Congo River had a unique way of dealing with offenders. When someone committed a misdemeanour, the chief called everyone back to the village from the fields. The chief's throne would be set up in the centre of the *kraal* and the people would come and sit together. All work ceased, the pounding of the rice, the preparation of meals, the tilling or harvesting in the fields. The offender would be brought to the middle of the assembled community. 'Now,' the chief would say, 'we will hear what everyone has to say about you. Each person should speak only good.' For as long as it took, the stories of the offender's goodness would be rehearsed until all had said their piece. When all had finished, hours or even days later, the chief would say: 'You are free to go. How can such a person as you do such a thing? How could he ever do again what he did?' Offenders would be embarrassed by the avalanche of goodness that came down on them.

I cannot vouch for the authenticity of the story, but it serves as a parable for the gospel in our times. Increasingly I find myself converted to what Bill Burrows has called 'a "wisdom" theology of evangelization'. Like me, he too fears for the Church that is obsessed with its own internal dynamics, its failure to reform itself, and yet its paradoxical conformity to modern culture. Burrows reflects:

> The challenge of the Gospel in our culture is rather more subtle and paradoxical than the progressives' seeming conviction that benighted conservatives, militarists, capitalists, sexists, and racists are the problem. The same is true of the right for whom a mini-millennium will have arrived when relativists, non-Bible-believers, modernists, socialists, universalists, feminists, and pacifists repent of their ways. If both groups could agree that evangelization is the process whereby God transforms human beings and enlists human help in transforming societies, they might also see that unexamined but fixed ideas of the direction that this transformation should go may also be dividing them from a God who generally surprises everyone when revealed.[23]

The *undersong* of conversion is in the end about how the gospel is lived. Of course, how it is understood determines to a degree how it is lived. At this point in my life the elements I have traced in this chapter are the substance of my conversion to date. It is both present moment and continuous experience.

3

THE UNDERSONG
OF COMMUNITY

A FEW MILES FROM BOSTON, MASSACHUSETTS, lies the beauty spot of Walden Pond. Here, in a small log cabin donated to him by the writer Ralph Waldo Emerson, the naturalist and philosopher Henry David Thoreau wrote his voluminous diaries. 'We are constantly invited to be what we are,' he once observed. Speaking about the cost of a thing, he reflected that 'it is the amount of what I will call "life" which is required to be exchanged for it.'

Walking around Walden Pond with Iain, my best friend from teenage years, we reflected together on the fifty or so years of our lives, and the extent to which the aspirations we had as young people had been reflected in our respective journeys since. In our teens we were members of all kinds of intense groups of equally committed young people, having almost intuitively recognized the significance of what the French philosopher Levinas calls 'the Other with a capital "O" '. Teenage years, at least when I was growing up, were full of *angst* and aspiration in almost equal quantity. They held within them what Dorothy Day calls 'the long loneliness', and we learned with her that 'the only solution is love that comes with community.'[1]

Before going to Cambridge, Iain headed off to Wiesbaden in Germany. For the three months he was away we wrote regularly, sharing our dreams of a new tomorrow, as well as the more mundane elements of our lives. I still have the half of the correspondence he wrote to me, not least because it somehow holds the authenticity of a particularly intense period of our journey of faith and life. We were both seeking our vocation, our calling. But also we were seeking a context, a community if you like, in which to both live and share our maturing faith and relationship with God.

Today Iain teaches primary health care at Harvard, having spent most of his life as a doctor working around the world in situations of great complexity and deprivation. His transitory life of international travel has led him to seek community and root in a large church in Park Street, Boston, where he is a deacon. My search for community has been equally transitory. My journey has been as a teacher, and subsequently a priest. In the journey there has been a desire to belong, to find a home, at times made difficult by the kind of mind and faith that cannot easily buy into the dogmatic, but which nevertheless has a certain longing and need for certainty. What neither Iain nor I have lost is that sense that our vocation has to do with the 'other'.

MOVING TOWARDS THE 'OTHER'

Levinas expresses something of what this means for me when he reflects,

> In longing, the "I" moves towards the "other" . . . the movement towards the other, instead of completing or contenting me, implicates me in a concurrence of circumstances which in a way did not concern me and ought to leave me indifferent: What in God's name was I looking for here? Where does the shock come from each time I indifferently pass others by? The relationship with the other calls me into question, strips me of myself time and time again, by showing me ever new resources. I did not know I was so rich, yet I no longer have the right to keep anything for myself.[2]

I confess to a certain idealism, even fantasy, about community. I want it both to 'complete' and 'content' me. I am not entirely penitent of it either, nor are the countless groups and religious orders that over the centuries have sought a more authentic way of living their faith. But Levinas points to some realities that are all too often missed in the desire for a more authentic communion

in the name of Jesus Christ. There is a 'longing' in which the 'I'
moves towards the 'other'. Often, as in the case of Iain and
myself, that led to an intense search for God together, a deep
commitment to one another and to the vision. But it also led into
a 'concurrence of circumstances which did not concern me and
ought to [have] left me indifferent.' By this, I mean being involved
in the 'other', whoever that might be, involves risk, misunder-
standing, hurt as well as intimacy, love and understanding. And
this for me is where Thoreau's issue of the moment of what is
called life 'that is required to be exchanged for it' comes into play.

I am often shocked by the indifference I experience in church.
I am shocked too at times by my own indifference. Then it is as if
reaching out for the 'other' is just too much, too costly. There are
times when I cannot bear the thought of another encounter,
another act of relating. I understand at such moments the degree
to which every encounter with another 'calls me into question,
[and] strips me of myself time and time again.' On other occasions
I need the 'other' to call me into question, not in a destructive
way, but one which opens me up to new insights and experience
and shows me, as Levinas has it, 'ever new resources'. I often
desire this, but find myself strangely reluctant to open myself to it.

The faith I was brought up in placed considerable emphasis on
sacrifice. I understood well that 'I no longer have the right to
keep anything for myself.' For the most part I did not feel
resentful about this. There was a passion to save the world that
somehow over-rode any loss I might have felt. It took me some
time to learn that 'I did not know I was so rich'! As I have looked
back, however, I have been made to face up to what this might
have cost me, or more significantly those closest to me, and for
whom I have borne some responsibility. I wonder whether
perhaps the teaching was deeply flawed, and that sacrifice was
demanded over love, not by God, but by those who sought to
interpret God to our young impressionable minds. I have learnt
since my engagement with Ignatian spirituality that, without
knowing both that one is loved by God and freely chooses to love
in return, sacrifice can only in the end bring resentment.

Ours is a world that needs to celebrate and discover in community both God's love and the possibility of loving.

Undoubtedly when it does, then we shall reconnect with the cost of such loving. The late Ulysses Dove, the African American choreographer who died of AIDS, wrote a series of dances for a ballet entitled *Dancing on the Front Porch of Heaven*. For me these four dances poignantly focus on our contemporary indifference towards the 'other', and invite re-evaluation. In the first, *Self Giving*, he sought to show the need for 'giving over a major part of ourselves to someone for care' as an essential 'given' in being human. In *Friendship*, he reflected that 'nothing can come between two people – not even death.' In *Loss*, he sought to celebrate and honour the sanctity of life, and invited us to recognize that 'the fact that they passed through this world was enough to make a ballet.' It calls for a universal recognition of the value of all human life. The final dance, *Letting the Skirts Go*, exposes the extent and necessity of love in the process of parting: 'they cannot go until they've been told they've been loved.' When the black teenager, Stephen Lawrence, was killed on the streets of South London, the woman who cradled him as he died murmured over and over again to him: 'You are loved, Stephen, you are loved.'

Caring, belonging, personal worth, and loving are all values of community which somehow find scant place in the dissonant world in which we live. To imagine for a moment that the malnourished child, the AIDS victim, the butchered corpses of another genocide who have passed through this world were 'enough to make a ballet', is mind-blowing. For we have lost the sense of celebrating and honouring the sanctity of life, or the ultimate value of 'giving over ourselves to someone for care'. To care is to speak to the longings that we feel, and to address the things that drive us crazy. And perhaps the thing that drives us most crazy is the need to be told that we are loved.

My search for community in which the elements of care, belonging, personal worth, loving and being loved are present has over the years taken me down some difficult paths. For the most part my experience of community, of belonging, has been, on the surface at least, a failure. Though, as a young lawyer I once met in a São Paolo *favela* acutely observed, 'success is never final – failure never fatal!' In each experience of 'community', whether short-lived or more long-term, I have learned much, and something in me still holds a longing for some tangible expression of what is perhaps more fantasy than reality.

Of course, the biggest block to community is the egotistical self. In my early days as a Christian I sought the perfect church, always wanting the next one to provide the things that the last one lacked. Fortunately, before my egocentricity finally conquered reason, a wise friend commented, 'Peter, if you find the perfect church, don't join – you'll spoil it!' So I became an Anglican!

THE COMMUNITY OF THE 'SELF'

The community of the self is both the most essential community to learn to live at ease with, and the most formidable. Coming to terms with the community of the self requires recognition of the complexity and nature of that self. Let me illustrate with this diagram:

I

I am

I am I

I am one

I am many

I am a community

of persons known, loved, hated.

Within me lives a collection of people

I have followed or fought, accepted or avoided,

chosen as good models, rejected as bad models,

prized, valued, idealised and/or disliked, devalued, despised.

They are all there, remembered or forgotten somewhere within.

I have learned from all of them, willingly or not.

I have grown from their gifts, good or bad.

I have gained much because they were there.

They are my teachers, my guides.

They make up my museum

my inner community

my community

of the spirit.

Because of

them all

I am

I[3]

The community of the inner self is the primary one in which to find personal worth, love, acceptance and care. By care I mean that 'paying attention' to the self that makes the healing of the self possible. We are what we are. As a friend has commented, 'What we shall become in the future has not yet been made known' – the influences and people that have taught and guided us in the positive dimensions of our life, those we have prized, valued and idealized. Yet they are no more important or significant than those whom we have fought, avoided, disliked, devalued or despised. Their place in our 'museum' or 'inner community' is of equal value. As someone of faith, it has taken me many years to discover the truth that it is the whole person that is seen by God to be of ultimate and infinite value. And if of such value and worth, then lovable and loved.

During the 1980s while a parish priest I was part of a small community of people who, while not living in the same house, nevertheless shared significant elements of their life: common meals, a commitment to sharing as truthfully about ourselves as we could, support of each other in social action, worship together several times a week, and the intention of living our lives more simply in favour of the poor. The experiment lasted some two years, and the journey was marked by times of great humour, fun and a sense of well-being, together with periods of pain, dissension and separation.

A number of years later I was to realize just how painful it had been for some. Someone I did not know very well quoted people with whom we had been involved in community in another place saying, 'Peter and his community ideas have totally ruined our life. He always leaves people high and dry after having encouraged and enthused them.' At the time the remarks hit me like a hammer blow and, while I probably stood guilty as charged, we were all adults and each had the freedom to choose to belong or not, and to choose their level of commitment.

INTIMACY IS THE FIRST LAW

What our experience of common life did reveal was that 'knowing the truth about ourselves makes us humble and open to the truth in the world.'[4] During one of the more hairy moments of our community life I gained one of those insights which at first glance is unwelcome, but which in the end turns out to be the life-saver. I discovered my fear of intimacy and yet, surprisingly, my longing for it. I found that whenever intimacy became a possibility, and openness began to happen, I was fine until something over which I felt vulnerable began to be touched upon. Then the inner devastation I experienced filled me with such a sense of worthlessness and rejection that I would lose all trust and belief in the love that the other person, or people, had previously professed and demonstrated.

At the time I was reading Henri Nouwen's book, *Clowning in Rome*, and found his experience almost matched mine. 'Often,' he said, 'those who are most sensitive to the fears and angers of our world, and seek most intensely for solutions, also experience most deeply a need for affection and tenderness that their community cannot satisfy.'[5] For as long as I can remember I have had a strong commitment to justice, peacemaking and reconciliation, but often have lived inconsistently in myself with these realities. The moment of discernment over the fear of intimacy led to something of a long journey in discovering a path to both the true nature of intimacy, and a deeper sense of forgiveness.

Of course moments of discernment or disclosure are often preluded by other insights. As I have said, during the late 1970s, together with our family, we were members of an intentional community at Scargill in North Yorkshire. Like later experiences, this time was not a period of ministry about which I am particularly proud. But here I glimpsed a truth about intimacy that is perhaps a key to understanding about how to live in community – namely the need for solitude. I discovered that taking time away to reflect, pray, write or think made possible a deeper intimacy when with others. Again I found Nouwen speaking to reality.

> Without solitude, we begin to cling to each other; we begin to worry about what we think and feel about each other; we quickly become suspicious of one another or irritated with each other; and we begin, often in unconscious ways, to scrutinize each other with tiring hyper-sensitivity. Without

solitude, shallow conflicts easily grow deep and cause painful wounds. Then "talking things out" can become a burdensome occupation, and daily life becomes so self-conscious that long-term living together is virtually impossible. Without solitude, we will always suffer from a gnawing question about more or less: "Does he love me more than she does? Is our love today less than it was yesterday?" These questions easily lead to division, tensions, apprehension and mutual irritability. Without solitude, communities quickly become cliques.[6]

In a sense intimacy is the first law. We build up our relationships from birth from that first law. By the grace of God, the revelations that come up from the ground of our experience and through our relationships reveal the primary law of love. The process whereby we discover the possibility of intimacy includes not only solitude, but transparency, honesty, and fidelity. The primary law of love invites us to transparency and honesty with our 'museum' or 'inner community' of 'people followed, or fought, accepted or avoided', to a place where none of the parties use or exploit the other. What prevents intimacy is the refusal to allow for the virtues of transparency and honesty to find their place over against the negative whispers of suspicion or fear, whether of failure, or of being found out. Strangely, when we refuse intimacy, we do actually cling to each other, but often in self-destructive ways, ways that feed off our fears, doubts, insecurities and suspicion.

One of the reasons why the quest for community has never left me is a belief that transparency and honesty are integral to the way in which people relate to one another. This, together with a commitment to fidelity, the working out of relationships, is ultimately freeing. Then, it seems to me, we have a glimpse of heaven. When people committed to each other practise this spirituality of discernment, pray, discuss, and practise openness, together with a willingness to share love, the true gift of grace is received. Then an eternal truth is revealed, that gratuitousness redeems the world.

Weakness is not something easily admitted to in our contemporary world, success being the prevailing doctrine, and failure its antithesis. In religious terms weakness is also often associated with not coming up to the mark, or failing to live up to some real or perceived expectation either of God or of some community or relationship. Occasionally this failing to 'meet the mark' is what might be called sinful, in that at some level or another it denies the worth or value of the 'other', whether that 'other' be an individual, group, nation, God or the created order itself. But weakness too can be associated with those hidden wounds of life which cause us to be resentful, angry, unforgiving.

FACING THE WOUNDS

In 1993 Dee and I were invited to lead a conference back at Scargill. This was the first time we had returned since our painful leaving some thirteen years before. We decided to take with us some strips of red bandaging for an exercise we thought might be helpful in exploring one of the themes – dealing with our wounds. We had been given the idea by Robert Bly, who had recounted how his friend, Douglas Von Koss, at a conference in San Francisco 'had handed out two or three thousand strips of red cloth, and asked each man to fasten or tie a red strip of cloth over any part of his body that had been wounded in some way, a broken bone, a knife wound – a scar.'

'Many men,' records Bly, 'needed ten or more strips. For some men, the entire right side of the body, head to ankle, was brilliant red; on others the red almost covered the head; for some both arms and legs. When the exercise was over the room was a sea of red.'[7] Our experience that summer at Scargill revealed a similar record of wounds. Using the exercise as a parable, we explored together the hidden wounds, the handicaps to wholeness of un-resolved anger, strained or broken relationships, the withholding of forgiveness.

I spoke of the ease with which we disguise our wounds, our handicaps, by telling the group of an encounter I had had several years before on a beach at Weymouth in the south of England. A large woman was playing with a beach ball together with her son, who was handicapped by a form of spasticity that led to almost total lack of co-ordination of the limbs. The ball was thrown first by the mother; the boy failed to catch it, and scrambled after it to retrieve it and throw it to his mother. She in turn failed to catch it, and so it went on. What made the event so observable, and ultimately so moving, was that the two of them were clearly having a good time: they laughed at each other, at the absurdity and yet the joy of the game. I found myself reflecting on how eager I am to hide the handicaps and dislocation in my own life, often transferring on to others my refusal to deal with them.

Although forgiveness is at the heart of the Christian message, on the surface it appears the virtue that is least practised. It often takes a crisis in our lives to make us face up to the places and people from which forgiveness is either not sought, or withheld. Today we need the grace of forgiveness to be exercised within the Church and society more than perhaps at any other time. The growing secularization of our society has led to a return and recourse to law to sort out the sins of humanity, and grace, particularly the grace of forgiveness, has all but disappeared. It is regrettable that within the Church, too, we have become more concerned about rights than right relationships; about rightness, than righteousness; about being right, than having the humility to see the 'other' for who they are, rather than what they are.

The Chinese language has a character for 'crisis' that sees it both as a moment of danger and of opportunity. When I was preparing for heart surgery I found myself realizing that this was such a moment: the 'danger' that I might not recover fully, or might even die; and the 'opportunity' to put right some wrongs, and to restore some relationships. For the most part this meant writing a few letters, making phone calls, asking for some forgivenesses. As I made my communion and received anointing prior to surgery I knew a lightness of spirit that made me wonder why it had all taken so long!

Of course, what lies at the heart of such reticence is the fear of weakness, of not being in control. More recently I have learned something more about forgiveness which has led me to think that, like Guinness, it is good for you – or at least for me. One of the Zen masters says, 'Forgiveness is our only function.' In other words, it is what we are here for. I am not much given to the self-help books that proliferate our shelves, nor to the television gurus who offer panaceas for society's ills, but the words of one such has impacted on me in a quite surprising way. Writing about our capacity to hold within ourselves hatred, anger and resentment, Philip McGraw observes, 'You have the ability to forgive those people, not as a gift to them, but as a gift to yourself.'[8]

To see forgiveness as a gift to oneself I have to confess has come as quite a revelation. I have known the spirituality to which McGraw refers: 'the power of forgiveness is the power to set yourself free from the bonds of hatred, anger and resentment.' Perhaps what came as the fresh revelation was the comment: 'Seize the power and rise above the pain. You are worth it, and everyone you love deserves it.' By practising forgiveness we do ourselves good, and by doing ourselves good, we find the capacity to love ourselves. And as Jesus certainly understood, loving the other, neighbour or enemy, is not seriously possible without love for ourselves.

'LIFE MUST BECOME A GIFT BEFORE IT CAN BECOME A TASK'

Eventually there must be a reaching out. The community of the self is ultimately dependent upon the community of the 'other'. As I reflect on 'the yearning [which] is both the beginning and ending of the story, both the pull and push of the journey' – the *undersong* as it relates to community – it seems to me that there is a need to recognize the truth that 'life must become a gift before it can become a task.'[9] When I look back over the forty years or so since I first became a Christian, I am conscious that perhaps what we did not discover in our early years was the appreciation of life as a gift. In the post-war years, war-weary parents whose dreams of youth had been so dramatically interrupted by the horrors of war anxiously sought fulfilment in their children. The requirement to achieve, to give back, to change the world – 'It's up to your generation now,' my father would say – all this removed from us the capacity in some degree to appreciate life as gift. Life was essentially task. I hasten to add that I do not say this by way of blame. It was the way things were. Add to it of course the heady mixture of a religion that speaks of sacrifice, of 'laying down life for one's friends', and 'putting others first', and the cocktail is complete. I recall a priest friend of mine remarking, 'I'm forty-five years of age, I've finally learnt how to dance and to get in touch with who I am and what I feel. I've come alive.'

BEGINNING WITH WHAT IS THERE

I too have learned how to dance, to get in touch with who I am. It has been a difficult journey at times. In assessing my experience of community, I sense that the anxiety that governed each experiment was borne out of this dichotomy of seeing life as task rather than gift. The desire to 'make it work' was always stronger than the desire to begin with what was given. Paolo Frière, the Brazilian educator, when he sought to describe his revolutionary methods of enabling illiterate adults to read and find empowerment, said, 'You begin with what is there.' Often what was 'given' were two refugees, one black person, one old person, someone who was sick. What would bring them together? A meal, yes, possibly; a common agenda; a candle, something that focuses. In such a gathering we might observe that the universe is somehow present, because there is a promise of something that is life giving. In such situations the edge of the world becomes the centre.

In 1987 I made my first visit to the Sojourners community in Washington, DC. I had my first insight into this capital of the free world from the perspective of the underside. Arriving late on a Friday night, I found myself on the Saturday morning in the basement of a building surrounded by post-dated supermarket food. This was the free food line. Members of the community gathered to be led in prayer by a remarkable African American woman, Mary Glover. 'Lord,' she prayed, 'we know that you will be coming through this line today, so help us to treat you well.'

It was this discernment of the 'other', and of Christ in the 'other', that undergirds the need for 'another kind of community'; and of treating the 'other' well. I remember the first person who came to me, and into whose hands I placed a bag of mushy strawberries, reminded me of my grandmother, and I realized that in the providence of God, somehow there was that affinity. In the simple act of placing in the hands, a bond was exposed, and the wider issue, essentially political, was raised – what if this were my grandmother? Would I tolerate the circumstances that had forced her into such penury? Would I rave and shout, demanding an end to the mechanistic systems that force people into such poverty and degradation?

CHOOSING OPENNESS TO THE 'OTHER'

So often, what opens us up in such circumstances is example – modelling of the alternative 'other'. A while later I was in Dublin visiting tenements on an estate gradually being demolished to provide smart apartments for the nouveau riche so that they could be near the banking and business centres of the city. With a friend we made our way across waste ground, already a 'no go area' for the police. Burnt-out buildings, derelict 'joy-ridden' cars, and an ever-present feeling of menace – and yet strangely we felt safe. We were accosted first by children demanding money, then by adults asking where we were going. When we replied, 'To see the Sisters', it was as if a spell had been broken; smiles wreathed faces, the children formed a procession and we were almost carried to the tiny apartment on the second floor where three members of a religious order had made their home.

The doors were open to all. Here anyone could come, sit around the kitchen table, share whatever was on it, pour out their troubles, and tell their own stories. Occasionally there would be Eucharist, no one was barred. Here, too, among the ordinary were the radicals, the movers and shakers making their home among the powerless and disempowered. There was Kevin – a man of indeterminate age, covered in tattoos, stubbled chin, who lived on his own and yet felt the 'need for community'. An activist committed to what he saw as 'biblical justice', he had spent the day demonstrating against a supermarket chain for its selling of South African produce – it was before the ending of apartheid. He had opposed the visit of President Ronald Reagan and boy-cotted McDonald's because of his perception of its policies on cattle raising in Latin America. When asked whether, if he were the only one to boycott something, it would be worth it, he replied that if you felt an action was right, then whether there were a hundred or just one, you had to act. Kevin belonged to a group of people stripped of most of their power by poverty, unemployment, and now homelessness. But somehow he refused not to be open to the 'other', tolerating difference, refusing to excommunicate.

That evening, sitting around the table, we listened as people faced the rawness, the questioning, their accounts of harassment and indifference. Then we listened to some stories from the older folk as they reminisced about what it had been like to live in the neighbourhood before the flats that were now being torn down were built. 'It was lovely here then,' they said, 'a village of white-washed cottages, a community.' After a while we watched a little filmstrip presentation – *The Stations of the Forest*. It was about the effect of the deforestation in Brazil, particularly upon the Yanomani people. Here in this utilitarian cosiness we were sharing something beyond words. In a few hours we had touched the heights and depths of human experience. We had wept together, laughed, and feasted together, as well as turning toward the 'other'. And it was so ordinary!

THE 'LITTLE VIRTUES'

I have often reflected that those of us in the Church who feel compelled at some level to share our faith with those outside of the Church miss so much. We seem to forget that 'mission is life, adaptation and sensitivity to the signs of the times.'[10] In the earliest days of Christian history, proselytizing others was a risky business. Modelling Christian behaviour was something which Christians who were often from the poorest social groups, artisans, soldiers and farm workers, had to find ways of doing. They learned to practise what have been called the 'little virtues' – gentleness, peace, humility, patience, temperance. These were often the most powerful outward signs of a lived faith in times when such behaviour was unusual. Christians were encouraged to share the ordinary things of life, meals, being helpful to others, not looking for advantage.[11]

In the little groups I have encountered in my travels I have witnessed much of this practice, and continue to do so day by day in encounters with people, as I seek company outside of the circle of the familiar. I am constantly surprised at the level of commitment to the 'other' from all kinds of groups of people. As I write these words I have just baptized and confirmed a black woman in her forties who is dying of cancer. Talking with her sister and others before the service, I was told of this woman's commitment to the 'Women Against Arms' campaign in South London, and her involvement with the Metropolitan Police and community 'Trident' campaign to rid the neighbourhood of drugs, guns and violence. 'When everyone else was afraid to speak up, she did,' reported her sister. Her priest spoke of her attendance over many years at funerals of those killed by violence, but how in recent weeks, with her cancer threatening her life, she had wanted to 'put things right with God'. Stories such as hers model an alternative behaviour witnessing to the 'little virtues' of perseverance, struggling with indifference, and a searching for peace.

In the moments of serendipity that such encounters reveal I find myself constantly confronting the reality of God at work in hidden ways, pursuing in ordinary people the kingdom of justice, love and peace. So often, however, our overt concern for making people fit into the structures of the Church, and the terminology of our faith, makes us blind to the reality of God's saving justice.

THE LOVE THAT COMES
WITH COMMUNITY

I have reflected a great deal in this chapter about the *undersong* of my experience of community, its ups and downs, the yearnings, and the fits and starts. However, the experience that was at the time the most frustrating also became the most fulfilling. It grew out of one of those moments that Paolo Frière referred to – by beginning with 'what was there.' A group of religious from a Catholic order had moved into the neighbourhood of one of south London's middle rise housing estates. Here in long low structures with many hidden corners, badly lit stairwells and endless windowless corridors, people lived forgotten by the authorities, except insofar as the residents were a problem. Together with the local Methodist minister and myself, a group of us formed to see whether we could facilitate something like one of the base Christian communities that flourished in similar circumstances in Latin America and elsewhere in the world. Some of the sisters had been working in Peru with such groups, and they believed that their vocation was to try and enable such communities in south London.

Over a number of months we gathered together people who described themselves as 'survivors' or 'refugees' from the different denominations who attended churches on the periphery of the estate. One woman – we'll call her Jasmin – known to many on the estate because of her friendly smile and willingness to engage with people, eventually offered her home for us to meet. For three years a group of us met most weeks to listen to each other's stories, to reflect on the Scripture, pray and see what difference we could make to the neighbourhood. In the early days the flats were plagued with little red ants that appeared in food tins, infested carpets and beds, and generally intimidated people by their apparent omnipresence. The group reflected on the Scriptures – not surprisingly the plagues in Exodus! More practically, they got together a petition to the local authority to have the estate disinfected. Names were collected and the authorities informed. Little happened. It seemed as if, as in so much else, these people were unseen and unheard.

After six months or so we began to give up, until someone asked if the disinfectant teams came, who would let them into their homes? Many people worked during the day. Someone asked, me I think, why not let someone who was not working have the key to their neighbour's apartment? There was real consternation. Burglaries and theft were rife on the estate, and when convictions were achieved it became clear that neighbours were often the thieves! We reflected again on the Scriptures, on passages like, 'The thief comes only to steal and kill and destroy. [Jesus says] I have come that they may have life and have it to the full.'[12] We asked what it would mean to have life *to the full?* It would mean trusting one another, they observed. Before long, someone offered to give their house key to a neighbour so that the deinfestation work could be done. It was a small but crucial step of trust. Here was a practical fulfilment of the commandment to 'love your neighbour'.

Sadly, of course, there were setbacks. One member of the group 'borrowed' the funds that had been collected to help start a children's project. We found facing into that crisis very hard indeed. But somehow for three marvellous years we struggled together to offer some kind of alternative to the isolation and lack of community, as well as to stem the tide of folk who just wanted 'to get out of here'. All sorts of people joined us, including the local chair of the housing association, who got little or no support from residents. He made no pretence to being Christian, but he was happy to fit into the pattern of community life with its prayer and Bible reflection, because he saw the group as a place of solidarity, committed to the same hopes for the welfare of the neighbourhood as he had.

What was 'given' here was pretty much Frière's two refugees, one black person, one old person, someone who is sick. The focus that brought them together was the common agenda of their isolation and lack of a sense of belonging. Here the edge of the world became, for a few brief moments a week, its centre. Our experience of community here lasted around three years. In it we learned a great deal of the *undersong* – the emotional current that carried us on; often that current was uncomfortable and the pull and push of the journey frequently threatened to pull it apart. Of course the fragility of the lives that people led, with all their insecurities of work, of home, of family, of personal safety, were sufficient in themselves to destroy things. But there was a time of grace, and a few weeks before I completed this chapter I was visited by someone who has begun again what we began ten and more years ago. As we talked, I recognized that God who is community, as Creator, Sustainer, Life-giver, was both the beginning and the continuing of the story.

4

THE UNDERSONG OF JUSTICE

In early September 1998 a Swissair jet airliner crashed into the sea off Nova Scotia. In the aftermath of the crash it was discovered that a large number of those on board who died were aid and charity workers. Among them was Pierre Gerety, described by *The Guardian* newspaper in an obituary as 'a Champion of the Poor'. Gerety had been legally trained at Harvard, and influenced from his childhood by the Jesuits. One of those paying tribute, Iain Levine, said of him, 'He was difficult to work with at times, but it was understood that this was because he set high standards. In negotiations he was never aggressive, but took the approach to certain things like human dignity – it was non negotiable.'

Something of Gerety's determination was echoed in his own words: 'If the law is on your side, argue the law. If the facts are on your side, argue the facts. If neither is on your side, take off your shoe and bang it on the table.' Gerety represented that rare group of people 'who carry us beyond kind words and good deeds for desperate people, beyond the kind of charity that makes the obscene palatable, to the kind of justice that makes the obscene impossible.'[1]

'THE MUSTARD SEED OF HOPE IN A CURABLE WORLD'

Over the years I have found the search for the 'kind of justice that makes the obscene impossible' requires what Pinchas Lapide[2] calls 'the mustard seed of hope in a curable world'. Such 'a mustard seed of hope' seems to me to call for a profound belief in a God who creates in order to provide joy, goodness, and a place for humanity to live in peace and safety.

I emphasize that I need a belief in God for this, because over the years of activism, in issues from nuclear disarmament to the search for reconciliation in Ireland, and an end to military oppression from Latin America to the Middle East, I have found that many who seek justice are not Christians, or people of religious conviction, but like Pierre Gerety take the approach to certain things like human dignity as being 'non-negotiable'.

Too often I have faced my own collusion with the 'kind of charity that makes the obscene palatable'. In part I believe this has been due to an inadequate understanding of sin, salvation and justice. For much of my journey, salvation has been over-personalized and individualistic, and justice has been something which will be meted out at the end of time, rather than a vision of a future of humanity living in peace and love. And if salvation has been over-personalized, then sin has too often been unrelated to the 'kind of justice that makes the obscene impossible'.

For the first Christians living in the Roman Empire salvation would have been a profoundly political term associated with the role of the emperor as 'saviour' – the one whose task it was to ensure the peace, security and welfare of citizens. To follow Jesus as Saviour was, for the fledging Christian communities, to challenge the power of the emperor. Jesus demanded an alternative allegiance, a new rule, and a new model of salvation, one in which justice, love and peace, energized by self-giving, forgiveness and reconciliation, would make possible a new order in which all humanity could live in harmony.

Like many contemporary Christians, I have been slow in coming to this recognition of the radical nature of following Jesus Christ. In 1980 I was spending a few days on the island of Cumbrae in the Clyde estuary in Scotland, trying to sort out some of the mess of my life in community, much of it caused by my own stubbornness and hardness of heart. Across the estuary lay the nuclear submarine base of Faslane – even with the naked eye it was possible to see the black shining whale-like monster submarines, and their busy attendant vessels tending to their murderous needs.

One day during my stay I picked up a copy of *Sojourners*, a magazine written and edited by a community of people working with the poor of Washington, DC. It was my first contact with a community that for nearly thirty years has sought to maintain a biblical perspective on the political, social and moral events of our time, and to discern the role of the Church in the world. At the time there was considerable focus on the nuclear arsenals held by the super-powers, and somewhat late in the day I had begun to wonder what relationship such issues had to my faith and understanding of God's purpose in the world. Within sight of the very weapons themselves across the bay, I found an article asking questions of nuclear weapons – 'Can the use of these weapons be reconciled with the gospel? Can their existence be reconciled with the command "Love your enemies"?'

It was a *kairos* moment for me. For years I had relied upon the arguments that we needed such weapons to ensure our security. I had allowed myself to believe the moral lie that 'if we are attacked we should retaliate.' Despite the fact that I had seen for over ten years on the streets of Belfast the practical futility of such arguments in a localized conflict with much less significant weapons, I had failed to grasp the horrendous implications for humanity of the unleashing of the nuclear weaponry whose transport systems I could see from my bedroom window. My theology of conversion and renewal stopped short on where I stood in relation to such issues. The question that now began pressing upon my conscience was, 'How can I as a Christian accept this situation?' On a more personal level, I found myself asking, 'What will it take for me to disarm unilaterally in relation to my enemies?'

A 'GERM OF HOLY DISCONTENT'

These moments on Cumbrae, together with times of disclosure on Belfast streets, and among the people of my first parish, provided somehow a 'germ of holy discontent'[3] which took root in my spirit and nudged me towards a re-evaluation of both faith and humanity, as well as the role and mission of the Church in the search for *God's* 'saving justice'.[4]

Eric Hobsbawm, a Marxist historian, observed on the fall of the Berlin Wall,

> We do not know where we are going. We only know that history brought us to this point . . . However, one thing is plain: if humanity is to have a recognizable future, it cannot be by prolonging the past, or the present. If we try to build the third millennium on that basis we shall fail. And the price of failure, that is to say the alternative to a changed society, is darkness.[5]

Hobsbawm spoke from a painful honesty about the failure of a cause,

> Much of my life, probably most of my conscious life, was devoted to a hope that has plainly been disappointed, and to a cause that has plainly failed: the communism initiated by the October Revolution.

When I first read this, I found myself deeply moved, not least because at times I have identified with his disappointment in the cause that for most of my conscious life I have been devoted to – the Christian faith. Like Hobsbawm, I do not think we have a future if we base it on the flawed interpretations of the Christian faith that have made collusion with war, violence, the oppression of women and the poor, so much a part of our failure to *seek justice*. Can we admit to failure? James Alison argues that 'being wrong can be forgiven; it is our insisting on being right that confirms our being bound in original murderous sin.'[6]

Unlike Hobsbawm, I do not believe that 'we do not know where we are going.' Both existentially and eschatologically I have a deep and profound hope in a God who will bring what is hidden to the light, and make right what has been wrong. But I am not naïve about this, neither am I of the view that it is something that we have to hold on to as some kind of utopian ideal. We can and must make a difference to the way things are in the here and now. But for many of us it requires a process of relearning. To learn, we have to unlearn; and to learn justice, we have to unlearn injustice.

Around the time Hobsbawm wrote about his disappointment at the failure of Communism, Pope John Paul II observed of that event, 'Now Communism has gone we have to be on the side of the poor, otherwise they will go undefended.' As I read these words, I was deeply saddened and angered a little, too. I railed inwardly, 'Just because Communism has gone – we have to be on the side of the poor! Surely that is the Christian vocation!' When I had simmered down, I thought again about what the Pope had said. How often in history has Christianity strayed from its true vocation and been offered the possibility of redemption by rediscovering it, and offering hope once again to the world. The Pope was reminding Christian people that their vocation is to defend the weak, and that in some way Communism provided both a judgement and a catalyst for the Church. The failure of the 'cause' of Communism provides an opportunity for relearning the way of justice.

How we relearn is of course critical. It begins with the virtue of acceptance. The acceptance of the 'other' – whether the other is 'enemy' or 'poor', 'male' or 'female', 'gay' or 'straight' – makes the true search for justice and the welcoming of the alternative rule of God possible. Most of the time our refusal to accept the 'other' is the refusal to accept the unacceptable in ourselves. Brendan Kennelly, an outstanding contemporary Irish poet, was holding a breakfast seminar for business and professional people. He sought to address the issue of acceptance. He told his distinguished audience the story of a young man who had worked on a building site. One day the young man fell and was so badly injured that he lost all feeling in his body except for a small area near his forehead and chin. In time he learned to use a computer with his mouth and wrote a book entitled *Just my Luck*. In it he told of his accident and about his loss of the sense of feeling, but of how in losing the physical sensation of feeling, he had discovered his emotional feelings, how to be sensitive, to cry and to love. The loss of physical feeling led him to the discovery of his emotions.

Kennelly asked his listeners to reflect on when they had last

expressed something of how they felt to themselves, to their
spouse, or a colleague or a friend – someone who needed to be
touched. By the end of the meeting men were hugging one
another, and weeping. A judge with his head in his hands said,
'How am I going to explain this to my wife?' Kennelly concluded,
'If for one second you let Christ into your life, it would transform
you. You would never be the same. And you just have, for Christ
comes to us when we allow ourselves to feel, to become caring
and compassionate. Such is his power.'[7]

The *undersong* of justice begins not with some great cause, but
rather in the simple acceptance of ourselves, and of others. In
such a way we rediscover the humanity in ourselves and in others
and can begin to show care and compassion, together with vulnerability. This is in part what it means to allow Christ to come to us.
Hobsbawm's desire for a 'changed society' is a deeply held
longing. The virtues integral to Christian belief and practice hold
within them the potential to offer hope, but they are all too rarely
self-evident in the ways in which institutional religion works.
Pope John Paul is right: 'we have to be on the side of the poor,
otherwise they will go undefended.' There is a need to rediscover
our vocation: that to be truly human is to be just.

TO BE TRULY HUMAN IS
TO BE JUST

Much of life is about discovering our calling, our vocation.
William Stringfellow, a lay theologian and Harvard-trained
lawyer, whose practice was among the poor of New York's Lower
East Side, understood it as follows: 'Vocation has to do with
recognizing life as gift and honouring the gift in living.' He understood, too, that 'being holy does not mean being perfect, but
being whole; it does not mean being exceptionally religious, or
being religious at all; it means being liberated from religiosity and
religious pietism of any sort; it does not mean being morally
better, it means being exemplary; it does not mean being godly,
but rather being truly human.'[8] To be truly human is to be just.

Ours is a world in which the recognition of life as gift has been
largely forgotten. The ease with which we accept the human

detritus of war, famine, poverty and other catastrophes, is indica-
tive of this. The sheer scale of the wastefulness of human life,
and our disregard, is mind-boggling. Many Christians will have
difficulty in accepting some of what Stringfellow says, particularly
when he describes the Christian vocation as 'being truly human'.
But it is our lack of attention to the gift of being human that has
lost us our sense of vocation to defend the weak. St Paul commends the idea of growing up into humanness as being part of the
Christian vocation, arguing that Christ himself was an exemplar
of what it is to be fully human.[9]

When we understand the vocation of being human as a calling
to live justly, then it means that we begin to perceive that there
are limits to the powers of governments and other juridical
authorities, including churches. It is about breaking the power of
history. Often we need stories to help us to understand this, and
to receive the 'germ of holy discontent'. 'I will tell you something
about stories,' says Leslie Marmion Silke. 'They aren't just enter-
tainment. Don't be fooled. They are all we have, you see, all we
have to fight off illness and death . . . Their evil is mighty but it
can't stand up to our stories. So they try to destroy the stories, to
let the stories be confused or forgotten. Because we would be
defenceless then.'[10]

In the search for justice, stories must be both listened to and
told. Many of today's conflicts were conceived out of a history
when the conquerors refused to understand the story of the
peoples whom they conquered then colonized. Seeking after
justice demands a willingness to understand the stories and cultures of those who have been marginalized by colonization,
slavery and exploitation. The search for justice is as much a
search for what it means to be human. The history of humanity's
inhumanity has been one of 'destroying' others' stories – from the
mythical Cain and Abel, through countless holocausts from then,
until whatever is currently being played on our television screens
as the most recent genocide. All too often what lies behind the
destruction of the 'stories' is misplaced use of power by those
entrusted with it.

Recently I have been influenced by the anthropologist and
filmmaker, Hugh Brody. In his book, *The Other Side of Eden*, he

explores with his readers his encounters with hunter-gatherers and farming communities in places as diverse as the Arctic and Africa, among aborigines in Australia, the central African plains and Alaska. The purpose of his many journeys has been a rethinking of what it means to be human.

Over many years Brody has lived with the Inuit, the group of tribes living in the Arctic regions. As a young explorer he set off with the intention of learning the language of a people who had fascinated him from his childhood. The Inuit, though subject to various periods of colonization over the centuries, have tenaciously held on to both their culture and language. Brody's teacher was a man in his sixties, Simon Anaviapik. Anaviapik not only offered him language lessons, but the opportunity to live as one of the Inuit among the extended family.

The learning of the language was in one sense the easy part, although Anaviapik refused to speak a word of English, or to spare Brody's blushes as he learned of the way in which words like 'fear', 'inequality', 'control', and 'vulnerability' had come to the Inuit as a result of colonization. Brody's learning was deemed complete when he had not only grasped the language, how to tell stories, and how to tease, but when he had completed a gruelling hunting trip in which all had nearly lost their lives. Brody reflected, 'When I had asked Anaviapik to teach me Inuit, and when he said he was eager to do so, I had thought we were talking about words and grammar, about speaking, while he had supposed we were talking about a way of being.'[11]

Stories like this one reveal the complexities of human existence, culture and language, as well as the impact of colonization and its contemporary counterpart, materialism. To truly understand and accept the 'other' is revealed as a profound grace. But I think such a 'way of being' is what Hobsbawm speaks of as necessary 'if humanity is to have a recognizable future'. We have all too much evidence of the darkness that is the alternative, the heightened racism, nationalism, inter-communal violence and of disregard for life as gift. The question for me is: can Christianity and the other world faiths accept and work together to rethink our 'way of being human'? We have the language. The Jewish word for righteousness[12] holds within it the idea that 'all our good deeds, from almsgiving to visiting the sick to self-sacrifice, are for the sake of a neighbour who is our brother or sister under God';[13] and that without the 'other', be it God or our neighbour, we are not complete human beings.

Language on its own will not do it; there has to be a rediscovery of the 'other' as neighbour.

LOVE DOES NOT DO WRONG TO A NEIGHBOUR

Some years ago, in my search for a 'way of being' that seeks this kind of 'righteousness', I discovered the story of André Trocmé and the communities of his parishioners in the Le Chambon region of France during the Second World War. It was a story that brought together the twin elements of 'the kind of justice that makes the obscene impossible' and the 'germ of holy discontent' that took place in France in the 1940s, when the 'story' of European Jewry was almost snuffed out.

Shortly after the fall of France, Trocmé was visited by a frightened Jewish family who sought refuge. Without hesitation he and his family took them in and hid them. This was to be the beginning of a long act of mercy by Trocmé and his parishioners. By the end of the war, several hundred Jewish families had been hidden by the faithful and courageous people of the villages. On many occasions the Gestapo and their Vichy equivalents, the Milice, raided homes and demanded the yielding up of the Jews. All demands were firmly but politely refused. Refusal was to invite a death sentence, yet miraculously only one or two people were transported to the death camps, and none of these were Jews.

Resistance of this order rarely happens without preparation. To understand it, it is necessary to hear the story of the Le Chambon community. One incident illustrates the story well:

> It was a rather cool day up there on the plateau, even though it was mid August. A Chambonnais gave a short talk on the thirteenth chapter of St Paul's Epistle to the Romans. It had to do with the respect due to the authorities. There is no copy of the speech, but the thirteenth chapter opens: "Let

every person be subject to the governing authorities . . .
therefore he who resists the authorities resists what God has
appointed." And it urges Christians to do their civic duties,
like paying taxes and honouring those to whom official
honour is due. But it goes on to say, "Owe no one anything,
except to love one another; for he who loves his neighbour
has fulfilled the law. The commandments, 'You shall not kill,
You shall not steal, You shall not covet', and any other
commandment, are summed up in this sentence, 'You shall
love your neighbour as yourself.' Love does not do wrong to
a neighbour." To anyone who knew the chapter – and the
people of Le Chambon knew it well – the ethic of neigh-
bourly love demanded not a bitter confrontation with the
government, but a perfunctory, minimal respect for the
"governing authorities", with a firm but quiet hint that there
are limits to that respect, limits set by the commandments
not to do wrong to a neighbour.[14]

The talk was given against the background of a threatened
deportation by the local Minister of Justice. In both a letter and
conversation with the minister, the pastor and some theological
students conveyed the following message: 'We feel obliged to tell
you that there are among us a certain number of Jews. But we
make no distinction between Jews and non-Jews. It is contrary to
the Gospel teaching.' When I first read this encounter I was open
mouthed with the profundity and yet simplicity of it. Intuitively I
found myself substituting for 'Jew' other false categories, ' Black',
'Romany', 'homosexual', 'women', 'poor' – and a hundred other
discriminated-against groups. Here was a 'new way of being', and
I was confronted with my own lack of courage.

'WOE TO OUR SOCIETY IF TO BE HUMAN
BECOMES AN HEROIC ACT'

Visiting Yad Vashem, the Holocaust memorial museum in Jerusalem, I walked along the tree-lined 'Avenue of the Righteous
Gentiles'. Included among the names are André Trocmé and the
people of Le Chambon. This memorial to those who were known

to have rescued or given shelter and succour to Jews fleeing Nazi persecution surprises, because comparatively few people are commemorated there, given the scale of the persecution. This thought had not escaped Elie Wiesel, whose words to a gathering of Righteous Gentiles I have already quoted in Chapter 1: 'Most who cared were simple people who didn't even know what they were doing was courageous; they didn't know their acts were heroic. They did it because it was the thing to do. And I felt then woe to our society if to be human becomes an heroic act.'[15]

The thirst for justice, righteousness, uprightness – call it what you will – is a fundamental requirement for the follower of Jesus[16] and the communities of faith to which they belong. As the Jesuit, Pedro Arrupe, has commented,

> In the church and preaching of the gospel message of justice and salvation, a denunciation of existing injustice is necessarily implied. Denunciation demands courage – often great courage. For to denounce an injustice will often mean to confront, perhaps to unmask, but in any case to contradict powerful men who control the levers of political power. And Christ our Lord, in the instructions he gave to his Apostles, has warned us what a risky thing it is to be a witness to the gospel. "They will hand you over to the Sanhedrin and scourge you in the synagogues. You will be dragged before governors and kings for my sake to bear witness before them and the pagans . . . do not be afraid of them."[17]

'THERE ARE LIMITS TO RESPECT FOR THE AUTHORITIES'

To behave in such a way for most middle-class Christians means undoing years of conditioning. Respect for authority is such an inbred discipline that to acknowledge, as the Chambonnais did, that 'there are limits to that respect' is in itself a paradigm shift that most simply cannot make. I remember my own dread of demonstrations: I would wake early, wishing as always that I hadn't agreed to yet another march. Somehow the idea of demonstrating, of being 'out front' on a political issue, was and still is alien to me. The police who were drafted in to marshal us were mostly courteous, friendly and rarely displayed the resentment I would have if my leave had been cancelled for yet another demo. I never felt triumphant or virtuous – just poverty-stricken, sinful and weak. Always the places of violence, compromise, fear and injustice were touched in me.

In more recent times that task of confronting, even unmasking injustice, has been done at a more face-to-face level with politicians and civil servants. Here one's vulnerability is truly exposed! People of my background in Western democracies are basically courteous and respectful of authority. The idea of disagreement, or the thought that something in a democracy could be unjust is, well – unthinkable! In the presence of the powerful, once the point is pressed, the frailty of one's case is exposed by the production of many more facts than you have at your command. Inevitably you feel you are about to be exposed as a charlatan, unreasonable – and maybe even a little mad. And believe me, by this stage in such encounters it is tempting to believe it – tempting to believe it oneself!

What makes seeking for justice such a difficult task for mainly white middle-class Christians goes beyond the struggle over 'limits to respect' and the need for unlearning elements of what is ingrained of both our faith and culture. For me the biggest single area of struggle has been that of accepting a lack of ability to effect change and yet somehow to keep working for it.

> Sharon Welch has raised this question in her *Ethics of Risk*, where she observes, 'Why is it that white, middle-class, socially aware people so often end up despairing over their lack of ability to effect changes in our socio-cultural, economic, and religious institutions?' Her answer is that members of the white, educated, middle-class want to see results: they measure their failures against the criteria of effectiveness; they want social programmes to work according to the ideals and goals motivating their actions. Over time, however, they begin to realize how ineffective their programmes and actions have been, how impossible their ideals and visions,

and this leads them to a 'cultured despair' and eventually to a 'giving up'.[18]

I understand this 'cultured despair', this 'giving up'. I have reached that point in my life where the measurement of achievement can be a depressing enterprise, as well as recognizing that there are profound limits both to energy and strength. There is also the painful realization that the world is much more awful than one could ever have imagined. But what has kept the *undersong* of justice alive in my spirit has been something of the reflection that Sharon Welch went on to make in what she calls the 'feminist ethic of risk'. Such an ethic she sees as retaining a commitment 'even and especially in the face of uncertainty, the lack of guarantees, and the knowledge that things may never change.' Like Welch, I have observed many women around the world in the townships and *favelas* of Africa, Asia and Latin America, for whom 'the luxury of despair and giving up is not an option for them. Theirs is an ethic of faithfulness rather than effectiveness . . . creating a matrix in which further reflection and action becomes possible, a heritage of resistance and hope.'[19]

Jesus' invitation to his followers to 'seek God's saving justice' does not carry with it any guarantees, any certainty of seeing its completion in our lifetime. As then, so now, we are often only witnesses to signs of its coming. When I was baptized at the age of fifteen, the pastor of the Baptist church to which I then belonged offered for my reflection the text in the Authorized Version of the Bible, 'He that is faithful in that which is least, is faithful also in much.'[20] I remember being quite disappointed: I felt it was a kind of judgement on me. I had wanted some more *macho* text, something like 'taking up the cross', or 'laying down' my life! But at this point in the journey I find something almost prophetic in that baptismal text. Life is so often about little things; about moment by moment faithfulness, whether in relationships or commitment to causes or issues that are somehow or another energized, or driven by the conviction borne of faith in the person of Jesus. It is the accumulation of fidelity to the *least* that makes the *much* possible. What was being nurtured in me then in the *undersong* of justice was the ethic of faithfulness.

Signs of encouragement in the struggle for justice are there to be seen. Over the years, as I have had to do with people in power and close to power, I am aware that what passes for certainty over actions is not often as solid as it first appears. This came home to me during a visit to the Vietnam War Memorial in Washington, DC, which is located on two adjacent sites. The first and 'unofficial' People's Memorial consists of several large black marble slabs engraved with the names of the dead and missing. It is in a small sunken garden, and when I visited it first, it was at sunset one fine summer evening. The memorial is a triumph of the people over the reluctant, not to say recalcitrant State, who wanted no public memorial to what was widely perceived as a national defeat. I was moved to see little groups of people stooping and searching over the endless list of names, looking for that of a loved one. Many sobbed or cried quietly in the comfort of companions. Others had brought paper and stone-rubbing graphite wedges to copy names to take home, or pass on to relatives and friends.

A little way away from the People's cenotaph, above the garden, stood the official memorial. This statue of anonymous soldiers in combat dress is in clear contrast to the list of recorded names. The faces of the soldiers gaze questioningly towards the marble plinths. Somehow the sculptor had captured the mood of many about the Vietnam venture. And hidden in the sculpture's faces are the questions, 'What was it for?' 'How was it worth it?' 'Did we know what was done?'

'PLEASE SIR, DON'T KILL ME!'

Oliver Stone, the filmmaker, has understood something of the dilemma that this and other wars have caused in recent times.[21] He reflected, 'In Vietnam, Americans killed for not much reason, were frightened, repelled and excited, and then went on, as people do with their lives – the search for meaning comes later and is often desperate. "You never fought the war. You weren't even there" one veteran screeches at another in *Born on the Fourth of July*.' Later, in a speech given through the chief character Sergeant Butler at a Thanksgiving Dinner in Texas,

Stone reflects, 'There was a time when American soldiers went into a village and all that the inhabitants could say was "Xing ong dung giet toi," – "Please sir, don't kill me!" I was there. We were there. Humanity was there and it mattered.' Martin Woollacott reflected that 'Stone's films say humanity matters. It is a thing worth saying.'

For me, the 'limits to respect' for the governing authorities have been particularly stretched in time of war, because I too believe that 'humanity matters'. I believe this, at least in part, because of the faith I have in the person of Jesus Christ. Contrary to popular perception, Jesus offered few direct moral commands, but among his few was the call to 'love your enemies, and pray for those who persecute you; so that you may be children of your Father in heaven, for he causes his sun to rise on the bad as well as the good, and sends down rain to fall on the upright and wicked alike.'[22] Those, like me, who see this as an immutable directive to non-violence, are often accused of being naïve. Jesus too faced such criticism; he was challenging the status quo that set the boundary at 'love of neighbour'. 'You have heard how it was said,' Jesus observed, 'You will love your neighbour and hate your enemy. But I say love your enemies . . .'[23] For Jesus, the seeking of justice called for a paradigm shift in human behaviour. I think that this is much more than simply a philosophical alternative. I am well into the second part of my life. I am conscious of the increasing, rather than decreasing 'search for meaning'. I have become aware of how many veterans of wars have sought out their erstwhile enemies in the hope of some understanding of the 'not much reason' – that heady blend of fear, excitement and disgust that accompanies the passion of war. I think Jesus understood that we will all have enough things to regret in the ordinary 'pull and push of the journey', without adding to them by permitting ourselves to hate, to turn neighbour into enemy, friend into foe.

This is the *undersong*, the 'mustard seed of hope in a curable world' – the beginning of the 'kind of justice that makes the obscene impossible'. It is borne out of the ethic of fidelity that does not submit to 'cultured despair' or 'giving up': that is the 'germ of holy discontent' – true righteousness.

5

THE UNDERSONG
OF PEACEMAKING

DURING 1999 I WAS INVITED TO BE AMONG a small delegation
that went to Iraq to assess the impact of economic and military
sanctions upon the people of what had become a pariah state. In
1990 Saddam Hussein, Iraq's president, had ordered the invasion
of a neighbour, the sheikhdom of Kuwait. Within weeks Western
nations and Arab states went to war with Iraq and eventually
drove its forces from Kuwait. The alliance inflicted what military
people call 'collateral damage' on Iraq's cities, as well as upon its
military installations and civilian utilities such as water, sewage,
and electricity. By the war's end a nation once on a par with the
West in its education, health care, and economic stability became
the subject of punitive sanctions that by our visit in 1999 had
reduced it to a fourth-world state. This condition was attended by
all the usual curses of poverty, sickness, disease, hunger, hardship
and disorder. It is not the purpose of this book to address the
'rights' and 'wrongs' of the situation as it prevailed then, and now,
at the time of writing. However, one of the events of that visit has
remained with me as something of a parable of the requirement
upon the followers of Jesus to be 'peacemakers'.

Throughout our visit we were accompanied by members of the
Iraqi security service, from car drivers to senior officials, some
with an international brief for what is usually known as spying.
The visit was not without its dangers, not without approbation;
neither the church leadership at home, nor the government were
overly enamoured of our visit. We were warned of being duped,

subjected to propaganda, misled and generally being made patsies of. We were aware of all these things, and all of them happened. At the same time we were able to catch a glimpse of a people reduced in their humanity by authorities both within and outside Iraq. We witnessed courage in the midst of adversity, as well as great kindness and appreciation. We saw Christians with as few resources as others working for their neighbours to ensure alleviation from hardship where possible. We witnessed implacability on behalf of the authorities, who had it in their power to make the lot of their people easier, but through callous self-regard refused.

'SWORDS INTO PLOUGHSHARES'

One lunch-time we had been invited to dine with a Christian family known to one of the members of our party. We arrived accompanied by our usual cadre of officials, and together with our drivers were a party of about fifteen people. Our host and his family invited us all in to eat. On previous days our drivers at least had sat out in their cars. All of us were treated to beers and cokes before sitting down around a huge table, in the centre of which was a large unleavened loaf of bread. We positioned ourselves around the table so that we could talk to the family and friends of our host. Our minders were somewhat nonplussed. Those responsible for taking notes found it hard to do so amid the hubbub of the meal and the warmth of hospitality offered. Beginning the meal, our host took the large loaf in his hands and broke it; offering each of us a piece, he bid us welcome and assured us of his protection. We all ate, friend, foe, believer, unbeliever, Muslim, Bahai, Christian, betrayer, betrayed.

Towards the end of the meal, where many little diversions had been employed to gain a surreptitious word to hear about things as they really were, the host invited me into his garden. 'We will have a few minutes,' he said, 'then we shall be followed.' We crossed the narrow road outside his house and opened a gate into a piece of wasteland, the site of a house bombed in the war. 'Here I am building a garden for peace,' said my companion. 'Come and sit down with me under the fig tree. One day we shall do this in peace, although I may not live to see it.' He shared in the few precious moments his concerns, his fears, his longings. Sure enough, we were soon interrupted by the ever inquisitive and watchful officials. I thought then of the vision enunciated by the prophet Micah, speaking of the peace of God:

> God will judge between many peoples
> and arbitrate between mighty nations.
> They will hammer their swords into ploughshares
> and their spears into billhooks.
> Nation will not lift sword against nation
> or ever again be trained to make war.

But the bit that really got the hairs on the back of my neck prickling was the almost exact representation of Micah's vision that we had just experienced:

> But each one will sit under his vine and fig tree
> with no one to trouble him . . .
> For all peoples go forward
> each in the name of its god,
> while we go forward in the name
>   of the Lord our God
> for ever and ever.[1]

In those few moments in the Baghdad suburb we had glimpsed something of the true nature of 'peace on earth and good will to all' of which St Luke speaks.

Peace-making is not the same as peace-loving. All of us love the idea of peace but, like anything worth having, it has to be made, often painfully, at cost, and accompanied by disappointment and at times a sense of futility. My own journey in peacemaking has reflected all these things. I am not by nature a peacemaker, more of an appeaser. I remember in my childhood we moved home every few years. It was unsettling, and the task of making new friends, marking out the turf where one would be safe, and trying to survive the fear of being bullied in the playground, or set upon by gangs in the street, demanded of me strategies for survival.

I felt afraid often; I think I was quite cowardly, and probably still am. It wasn't that I didn't hit back, all too often I did. I remember in my first secondary school the usual initiations beloved of schoolboys were being applied by the bullies to the new kids. My turn came, and the meanest bully seemed to have been assigned to me. He was actually shorter than me. Friends evaporated as he approached, then, as they say, I 'stuck one on him' before he could attack. His surprise was total, as indeed was mine, and it was even further compounded by my offering to shake his hand. Suddenly we were surrounded, friends rematerialized; a crowd gathered, a fight usually followed. It didn't. The bully shook hands and departed with his supporters. It wasn't a lesson in peacemaking, more survival, but I learned in it something about the issue of 'demonizing' others, and the need for us all to make space for one another in this crazy world of ours.

INTO THE HEART OF CONFLICT

Peacemaking is a process that always leads those who would be peacemakers into the heart of the conflict. When I married Dee, who comes from Northern Ireland, the first rumblings of the years of violence that have marred Ireland for the past thirty or so years were being heard. The Civil Rights movement was gathering momentum, and for a while it looked as if some of the real inequities experienced by Catholics and the poor working class of both communities would be addressed. It was not to be. I remember sitting in my parents-in-law's home in Omagh in 1968 and hearing the first bomb go off. It killed the local residential magistrate. Thirty years later I was making a phone call home from a little village in Donegal. I heard the person in the next kiosk ask, 'Were there any casualties?' In a few moments I discovered that he was referring to the Real IRA bomb that had killed over twenty people and maimed hundreds of others, again in Omagh.

These murderous activities were both in their own way defining moments. The first, for me at least, became the starting point for my own involvement in peacemaking. A few weeks before we were married, Dee was walking in the Markets area of Belfast. A man approached her out of the crowd. 'Good morning,' he said,

'You look very happy. You will marry soon and your husband will be a healer. Goodbye.' And he went on his way. At the time I don't think either of us gave much thought to this, but as our involvement with the challenges of peacemaking deepened, it seemed as if this unsought-for intervention by this stranger took on a prophetic form.

I want to say at this point that my peacemaking activity has rarely been high profile; yes, occasionally I have been asked to say a few words on television, or contribute some remark to a radio news programme or newspaper. I have written several articles for journals, both Christian and secular, but in essence much of my involvement has been low key: informal meetings with groups of people from the peace line in Belfast, to the hill country of El Salvador, and the high density townships of Southern Africa. It has been a work of encouraging others, being alongside, listening to and being the confidante of those whose daily task is dealing with the violence, threats and intimidation, but with the resolve to be peacemakers. At the same time I have little doubt that it is a calling in some small way.

The Omagh bombing of 1998 was a defining moment in another sense: it brought together in a way that no other atrocity has done all but the most extreme of the warring factions. Because of our family involvement, as well as our commitment to peacemaking in Northern Ireland, George Carey, the Archbishop of Canterbury, asked Dee and me to represent him at the memorial service held in Omagh a week after the bomb. Prior to the event a reception was held in the civic centre for relatives of the bereaved and injured, visiting dignitaries, and politicians. Here, under one roof, were gathered friend and foe alike. It was not an easy time and space, but it was profoundly significant. My wife and I shuttled backwards and forwards across the room, talking with this group and that, as well as representatives from Sinn Fein and the Unionist political parties.

Catching sight of Martin McGuinness of Sinn Fein, a group of my mother-in-law's neighbours who had lost loved ones in the bombing expressed their anger at his presence. But this bomb had been indiscriminatory in a way that few others had – its shrapnel had sliced into the heart of all communities. When I spoke with

McGuinness, no stranger to violence, he told me that nothing would put him off the search for peace, and offered the reflection, as others on all sides, that this atrocity was a defining moment for the whole of society. Many commented at the time that Ireland was staring into an abyss.

Sadly, at the point of writing the peace process has not been fully implemented. For a brief moment I saw this abyss, in my own mind, as a deep well, yet shallow enough to catch a glimpse of our reflection in the water at the bottom. The Omagh bomb was somehow a culmination of the futility of hatred and the futility of violence in achieving anything good. Peacemaking takes peacemakers to the heart of conflict, but it must first take them into their own inner conflict. My own life has not been one of tranquillity and lack of controversy. In many ways I enjoy a good fight! Being someone of strong opinions, as well as a certain idealism, I find plenty of ground for destructive activity. Good friends frequently observe how much I need the wisdom of that anonymous quote:

> To war with oneself
> is the hardest war;
> to conquer oneself
> is the finest victory.

ON NOT BEING DIFFERENT...

In the aftermath of a particularly painful time of conflict and anger within my own relationships with others in shared ministry, a time when it was more important to 'be right' than to love, I found myself deeply touched by some words of Thomas Merton. Writing about spiritual pride and the danger of becoming isolated in self-satisfaction, of thinking of oneself as a 'prophet of God', or a man with a mission to reform the world, he remarked, 'I must look for my identity somehow, not only in God, but in other men. I will never be able to find myself if I isolate myself from the rest of mankind as if I were a different kind of being.'[2]

When I was growing up, my father was an officer in the Royal Artillery. I remember how often we were reminded that we had to behave in a particular way because of this. The implication was that somehow our father's rank put us 'above' others in some way. It has been one of the greater struggles of my own faith journey not to bring this attitude somehow into the way I think as a Christian. In my teens and early twenties I was particularly active in pursuit of a certain kind of holiness. I prayed a great deal, read the Bible, and was somewhat overscrupulous in dealing with sin, particularly my own. One day my mother, probably tired of my self-righteous piety, said sarcastically, 'I wish I could be as good as you are, but somehow my life doesn't make that possible.' The words stung, as I suspect they were intended.

Because the Christian faith is an evangelizing one, there is always the danger of arrogance, of seeing it as being 'better' than other faiths, rather than offering to the world a unique insight into the humility and humanity of God. For me, the cocktail of a certain arrogance of class, together with a culture of 'being different' as a Christian – combined with a personal lack of humility, which desires to be 'above' one's peers in some way, even as a minister of the gospel – all too easily creates an environment in which hostility, conflict, and even violence can emerge.

'EVERYTHING CHANGES ... EXCEPT OUR WAY OF THINKING'

In the *undersong* of peacemaking there are no short cuts, nor is there avoidance of dealing with the self. Thomas Merton again understood this, and some other words of his led me into recognizing the full force of what it means to be a peacemaker:

> So instead of loving what you think is peace, love other men and love God above all. And instead of hating people you think are war makers, hate the appetites and disorder in your own soul that are the causes of war. If you love peace, then hate injustice, hate tyranny, hate greed – but hate these things in *yourself*, not in another.[3]

I remember a friend commenting, 'There is enough anger in the peace movement to start the third world war all by itself.' Like many people, my involvement in peacemaking began as an

external activity. As others of the sixties generation, I had listened to Arlo Guthrie's parody on war, *Alice's Restaurant*, and
because like him I wanted to 'end war and stuff', I learned to 'sing
loud', as Bob Dylan, Joan Baez and other war-hating artists bade
us! But what for me began as an external issue became both
internal and external. I recognized how much within me was, and
still is, self-centred, self-destructive, and how much I shared with
a God-hating humanity who needed to rediscover, and re-engage
with a love-centred, life-saving, humanity-loving God in a deeply
personal way.

Gradually it began to dawn on me how radical and counter-
cultural is Jesus' instruction to 'love your enemies'. The over-
personalization of religion has given many of us the opportunity
to deal with it in terms of the petty enmity that emerges between
people in the ordinary intercourse of life. Of course dealing with
that is important in gospel terms. But the experience of dealing
with enemies who are created often for us on behalf of the state
for economic, political or other interests rarely engages the
Christian community. This has been particularly true over nuclear
weapons. We have lived the lie that they will not be used. But
they already have been, and with devastating effect, first at Hiro-
shima and Nagasaki; but in more recent times in more contained
forms in the Gulf War, and the Balkans, with the use of depleted
uranium.

From time to time individuals and institutions have dealt with
the matter notably and nobly. Einstein wrote, 'When we released
the energy from the atom, everything changed except our way of
thinking.' Because of that, we drift towards unparalleled disaster.
The compilers of Vatican II said that the dangers of world
destruction through nuclear weapons 'compel us to undertake an
evaluation of war with an entirely new attitude.' Billy Graham,
the evangelist, experienced a 'change of heart' following a visit to
Auschwitz and asked, 'Is a nuclear holocaust inevitable if the
arms race is not stopped?' Frankly, the answer is almost certainly
yes . . . I think many Christians are only beginning to see that the
nuclear arms race is an entirely new factor in human history, and
that we cannot be complacent about it, nor treat it as just another

minor issue. We need to educate the Christian community about the moral and ethical issues that are involved.[4]

A CALL TO FAITHFULNESS

Just how urgent such education is, was to my mind reflected in the 1998 Lambeth Conference, which was the first in many decades not to make a condemnation of the practice of war in general. In the 1980s the Sojourners community in Washington issued, together with other Christian bodies in the United States, *A Call to Faithfulness*. It was a document that demanded:

> the Church's preaching of the gospel in our day must make it clear that a turn to Christ will lead from the acceptance of nuclear weapons, so that converts will be known as peace-makers. The Church's public witness must be marked by costly action, following the leadership of one who was willing to bear the burden of peacemaking in a hostile world. Nurtured by Christ's love, his Church must "bear all things, believe all things, endure all things."

Such a 'call' takes us into the realm of the political, and here there is great resistance within all church traditions. Yet at the same time it is noticeable, in Britain at least, how the Church's approval, or at least tacit support, is frequently sought, and even expected in times of conflict. I have always found this difficult, because it seems to me that in every situation in which nations are required to intervene the circumstances differ. All too often intervention and the accompanying violence do not produce the intended outcome. There is a danger of oversimplification of course, but there is little doubt that the massive and unrestricted arms trade has made the task of peacemaking using other means much more difficult, and yet essential. Simply, peacemaking is at the heart of the gospel. We do violence to the message of Jesus when we only see its imperatives in terms of personal peace-making. Jesus, within his context, understood the alternative to Rome's empire as God's empire, and his teaching both resisted and exposed the violent and oppressive ways of empires. He hardly expects less of his followers.

If a point of conflict were reached where the major nuclear arsenals still held in various states of readiness by the world powers were to be deployed, at some point we would have to imagine the following scenario. On the first post-nuclear morning, when the enemies of the world had destroyed themselves, not to mention their neighbours, Christ would stand at that point in history and say, 'Did you have any part in helping to destroy all my children?' Perhaps the excuses would come, 'Well, what could we have done? Everything was so complex. We were helpless; we trusted those in authority. I suppose we helped to pay for the weapons, but surely you said, "Give to Caesar the things that are Caesar's . . . ".' And Jesus might answer, 'Verily, I say unto you, anything you did unto the least of my brothers and sisters, you did it unto me.'

A church committed to peacemaking is a church committed to the vision of Christ for humanity. On the eve of the Gulf War in 1990 I petitioned the then Archbishop of Canterbury, Robert Runcie, to join with the Presiding Bishop of the Episcopal Church in the United States, Ed Browning, and other church leaders in going to Iraq to seek an alternative to war. Robert Runcie was as always courteous and thoughtful. He replied to each of my petitions with great grace, but in the end said that he did not feel he could be party to such an act. Those who went included Jim Wallis, and he told me then that he believed that Runcie's presence might well have significantly changed the situation. Some years later, after his retirement, the former Archbishop was speaking on peacemaking at a gathering of the North Atlantic Association. I was an invited guest. I reminded him of our correspondence and conversations over this time. With great warmth and humanity, so typical of the man, he responded that people like me should continue to 'batter the gates' and not underestimate the influence upon conscience, and indeed the thinking, the voice for peace made.

'BE A ONE PER CENT PEACEMAKER'

During the Gulf War one of our neighbours was a senior civil servant deeply involved in the management of the war on a day-by-day level. We were good friends. Dee, my wife, had brought her own gentle voice of protest to our somewhat secluded mews of politicians and church leaders. At the time I was Canon Chancellor of Southwark Cathedral in London. When war was announced, Dee, who had been deeply affected by the announcement, resolved to light a candle every night for the duration of the war in the window of our second-floor lounge as covenant that she would pray. Her prayer was that God would save the life of one non-combatant each day. A neighbour living opposite, the wife of a senior politician, asked what the candle was for, and on hearing resolved to do the same. For several nights the two candles blinked at each other across the close at dusk. Soon, the wife of the civil servant asked what these two candles were for – and when she was told, she replied, 'I cannot light the candle because of my husband's job, but l will say the prayer.' 'In peacemaking,' says my friend David Bleakley, a stalwart peacemaker in Northern Ireland, 'give them an offer they cannot refuse. Be a one per cent peacemaker.'

This story has a number of strands. At the time I was involved with a housing estate in Peckham, where we had a small group working for the welfare of the neighbourhood. It was composed of people whose family roots were from all over the world. One night early in the war a woman came to the meeting whose mother had been staying with her sister in Riyadh. It was the first night of the Iraqi 'Scud' missile attacks on the city, and this woman's mother had been staying in a block of flats that had been hit by the first of these rockets to be fired. By some miracle no one had been injured or killed. I told Dee of course, and we laughed. Neither of us had believed that we would have any evidence of the covenanted prayer of the lit candle being answered, and there it was found among some of the people who were struggling most in our society to find a place, and hope for the future.

The second strand lay in the fact that after the dusk vigil of candle lighting had become known, and many joined in around the neighbourhood, our civil servant neighbour would regularly, when the demands of the war permitted, invite us in for a drink in the late evening. Together we would discuss the war; of course we disagreed, and yet at the same time we recognized how our respective positions had faced us both with difficult decisions. In the Church there was far from unanimity that the war was wrong; and in the nation equal ambivalence that it was right. On the night of 14 February 1991, when the allies bombed the Amirya shelter in Baghdad, it was full of men, women and children. Controversy surrounded the bombing immediately. Some apologists said that the building was believed to have been a missile site; others that it was an attempt to kill Saddam Hussein, who was alleged to hide in the shelters with his people during bombing raids. Neither seemed convincing, and having seen a number of these shelters in Baghdad in the suburbs, I remain sceptical. However, the night of the raid we had our usual late night drink with our neighbours. On the way in Dee said, reminiscent of John Cleese in *Fawlty Towers*, 'Don't talk about the war.' I replied, 'I won't if he won't.' Our neighbour opened the door – 'We didn't do it!' he said before the door was barely open. 'I didn't say anything!' I said.

'IT IS MIDNIGHT IN THE MORAL ORDER . . . '

There was little doubt that this was a defining moment. Consciences were tender and real anxiety was emerging about the outcome and the nature of the conflict. When during my visit to Iraq some eight years later I was taken to the Amirya shelter, I realized something of the full horror of the incident. The rocket had come straight through the roof, creating temperatures of 4000 degrees centigrade. Upstairs the people had literally been consumed; but downstairs, where the boilers were for maintaining the washing, cooking and cleaning of the shelter, people had been boiled alive. As the warden, Om Ghicken, showed us around upstairs in the blackened hall, I came across an image I will never forget. Etched like an ektachrome negative by the enormous flash that preceded the explosion was the outline of a woman holding her child milliseconds before their death. The shape of the outline was that universal image of mother and child, and reminded me of the Mary and Jesus Christmas cards that adorn our mantels inscribed 'Peace on earth'.

On the eve of the Gulf War I wrote in my Commonplace Book some words of Martin Luther-King: 'It is midnight in the moral order – there is a knock on the door of mankind.' During that most bloody of centuries, the twentieth, the Church's complicity in war was considerable. That isn't to say that there were not many contrary voices, nor that the complicity was without soul-searching, but in most of the conflicts from the beginning of the century it was 'voices within' rather than 'the voice of' the Churches that spoke out against the conflicts that led to a hundred thousand holocausts. As the ties of institutional religion become looser, the essential need is for a Church that under-stands and re-interprets for our times the gospel of Jesus in respect of peacemaking, and an end to the culture of hatred and violence that mark the human condition.

Many of us are witnessing the 'last of' commemorations of old combatants meeting to commemorate battles of fifty and more years ago. Few demonstrate any sense of personal hatred. Many speak of being caught up in the ideologies that captured their loyalty and forced them to arms. Thomas Merton saw much of what leads us into violence as being to do with hatred which is 'the sign and expression of loneliness, of unworthiness, of insuf-ficiency. And insofar as each one of us is lonely, is unworthy, each one hates himself.'[5] I believe that, albeit unwittingly, much interpretation of the Christian gospel has contributed signifi-cantly to the undercurrent that makes for war and violence. Our emphasis on human sinfulness, 'total depravity' as some theo-logians have it, can lead to a destructive form of self-hatred. We who hate ourselves recognize our self-hatred, punish ourselves continuously, bemoaning our unworthiness. And often we turn that punishment on to others, at its most extreme condemning others to hell in a moral, if not in a literal, sense. 'Punishment,' observed Merton, 'cannot cure the feeling that we are unworthy.'

Some of us have a strong hatred, the sort of hatred that 'takes joy in hating, because it does not believe itself to be unworthy and alone. It feels the support of a justifying God, an idol of war, an avenging and destroying spirit.'[6] Too often the Christian

Church has forgotten that 'from such blood-drinking gods the human race was once liberated, with great toil and terrible sorrow, by the death of a God who delivered Himself to the Cross and suffered the pathological cruelty of His own creatures out of pity for them.'[7]

'THE TERRIBLE RESPONSIBILITY OF THE DECISION TO LOVE'

There is a sense in which this is 'midnight in the moral order'. We cannot make the twenty-first century one that repeats the complicity in violence of the twentieth. The re-interpretation of the gospel is nothing less than a return to fundamentals. All of us find it easier to serve the hate gods because they feed all too easily on our capacity for a collective passion that blinds us to the awful realities of war and violence. There is a need to recognize the freedom with which Christ has set humanity free, offering us again what Merton calls, 'the terrible responsibility of the decision to love *in spite of all unworthiness*, whether in oneself or in one's neighbour.'

One thing I have learned in my struggles through the *undersong* of peacemaking is that there is no room for smugness or self-righteousness. I well remember completing my first article on peacemaking for a magazine and showing it to my father. He was deeply wounded by it because, although this was never my intention, he saw it as an attack on people like him who had fought in wars. He rightly observed that I had never had in reality to make the hard decisions against the real possibility of conflict. I had to agree, and I am saddened, because the issue was never fully resolved between us. A deeply Christian man, he was essentially a 'just warrior'.

For 'just warriors' and peacemakers alike there is a need for re-evaluating the gospel in our day, so that converts to Christ will be known as peacemakers. I believe that this task must be borne by the leaders of our Churches, and in the terms of *A Call to Faithfulness*, 'following the leadership of one who was willing to bear the burden of peacemaking in a hostile world.' The *undersong* of peacemaking is always prayer; as St Dorotheus of Gaza reflected, 'he who prays for his enemies cannot be vengeful'. Within this bidding lies the basis of communication. So often what makes for enmity in human relationships is the lack of communication. 'The incommunicable is the source of all violence,' observed John-Paul Sartre. Rather more chillingly, Wole Soyinka has reflected that 'those who make peaceful change impossible make violent change inevitable.' Simply put in this mnemonic is the path to peacemaking:

> Pray peace
> Think peace
> Speak peace
> Act peace

6

THE UNDERSONG
OF POVERTY

THERE HAD BEEN A FIRE IN the *favela*, and many people had lost all their possessions. The flames and smoke from the fire had been visible over much of the city of São Paolo. I stood surveying the ruins with Juan António, who along with others had been trying to help the residents of the shanty town to organize their lives, to obtain some of the basics that make life possible: water, sanitation and some health care for their children. 'If you can no longer dream,' said Juan António, 'God disappears from your heart.'

Earlier on that day we had spent time trying to get an audience with the local mayor. Every week over many years small groups of people including Juan António had been struggling with the authorities to obtain basic human rights for the *favelistas*, by presenting themselves at the office of the mayor. Someone had said, 'They will see us today because we have you with us.' They were right. The party was received, there was conviviality on behalf of the mayor, promises were made. 'Yes, there will be water, and prefabricated buildings . . . Of course, by this time next week.' We left, and when I enquired over a year later what had happened, the reply came simply, 'Nothing.' Having the dream of even the most basic things in life, and failing to see them delivered day after day, week after week, year after year, is it any wonder that God disappears from the heart?

My journey into the *undersong* of poverty is very much at the beginning. I still belong too easily to the religion that makes life comfortable, and that wants what Joan Chittister has called 'private consolation, rather than a religion based on the kind of public commitment that brings inequity into question.'[1] Certainly upbringing and education have contributed to a view of life that all too easily falls into stereotyping the poor as 'people causing trouble', indolent, lazy and dependent. Of course the reality is different. Among my earliest encounters with poverty in any systemic and systematic way was in the periphery of large Latin American cities. Here, in the 1980s at least, I met with small, determined groups of people whose personal stories of ill-treatment, enforced exile and social dislocation should break the hardest heart, yet who nevertheless refused to see themselves as victim, and whose activities and chief end were for the betterment of their neighbourhood, with all its inadequacies.

FOR 'US' NOT FOR 'ME' – THE 'MORAL AGENT' OF THE POOR

Their experience was illustrated for me in a kind of parable. Standing under one of the many road bridges that brought traffic thundering into the city, I was with a group of families whose homes had been made under the deafening roar of incessant lorries passing above them. People underneath lived in shacks, with wires looped from the power cables that had been illegally tapped to provide electricity for the dwellings. Children ran about, the ground was rock hard, concreted over; and yet in the middle was a tree, a bean plant, with its leaves, two of them: a sign of faith, of hope. 'Here,' said my friend Pat Clarke, 'people "waste time" helping their neighbours, carrying the loads of the elderly and infirm, being community.' The bean plant, surviving against the odds, symbolized somehow the ever-present possibility of new life, renewed humanity.

Such encounters bring 'inequity into question', make me face how little it takes to kill 'the dream' that Juan António spoke about, and make me realize how quickly 'God disappears from the heart.' I began to learn the extent to which the poor are what Harvey Cox called the 'moral agent' in a lecture I once heard him give at Harvard. Cox was reflecting on that extraordinary story

that Jesus told about the invitees to a wedding.[2] One was thrown
out because he did not have a wedding garment. 'Jesus,' said Cox,
'draws attention to the moral agent. He draws attention to those
who are present and the world that they inhabit. He says to the
poor, the sick, the moral outsider – you do not need to think of
yourself as victim. They become the "moral agent".' Cox concluded with a question: 'Perhaps the one who is told to leave is
the one who cannot see the change in status that the kingdom to
be brings?'

The effect of the poor as 'moral agent' has in a small part
brought me back to the values that our sophisticated society,
bombarded as it is by endless stimuli, has lost. These are the
values of neighbourliness, caring, awareness of the other, seeing
time as gift rather than commodity. Among the poor, such
perspectives are instilled in the young, too. Here is an example:

> The littlest learn from an early age. Whenever one offers a
> piece of hard candy or a tiny trinket to one child or another,
> a question arises inevitably: "But Hermana (sister), what
> about my little brother?" Even more poignantly, once, on a
> class trip, the donated picnic lunches – one for each of the
> poor youngsters – included more than one sandwich and one
> cookie. None of the children ate more than half of what
> had been given. Someone's enquiry about the mysterious
> uneaten half brought to the surface the appallingly obvious
> comment from an eleven year old: "Hermana, the other part
> is to share with the family at home." So much for individu-
> alism! Survival means "us" not "me". Together we survive
> in the search for life. "Doing one's own thing" at the expense
> of the rest spells only one word – death. "Without each
> other we are doomed" expresses the reigning ethic. The
> preferential option of poor people, even children, is "for us"
> not "for me".[3]

It is this sense of 'for us', rather than 'for me', that some of the
most liberating moments of my encounters with poor people have
opened up. A sort of learning of the reality that 'what for us is
upside down is right side up for other people.'[4] These are some of
the 'upside down' values of the significant 'other': the sharing

of resources, the non-dependence on possessions, and the refusal to commodify time. But it is in the arena of faith that I have found myself most humbled. Juan António's despairing comment at the site of the *favela* fire was actually unusual, while being totally understandable. For him, that tragedy in which he had lost loved ones was a 'last straw' moment. When I saw him days later, he had girded up his loins and started tackling the struggle again.

'WE HAVE BEEN CHANGED BY THE POOR'

Dick Junkin, who worked for many years as a Protestant missionary in Central America, was reflecting with a group of us one day during a visit to Salem, Massachusetts. He talked about how in Protestant theology three traditional 'means of grace' are recognized: *word*, *sacrament* and *prayer*. 'In Central America,' he observed, 'we have been changed by the poor, the hurting ones. We have learnt that there are certain "non traditional means of grace." These spring from the beatitudes – "Blessed are you poor". We learned that working with ex-offenders as a church community, being in regular contact with them, listening, letting them speak to our hearts, was a "means of grace". So with others on the margins of society we saw the need for boundaries to be examined.'

WORD – 'MADE FLESH'

It is learning from these 'non traditional means of grace' – the people, their circumstances, their story – that has enabled me to begin to see things from 'upside down'. But, as Junkin observes, the traditional means of grace, 'word', 'sacrament' and 'prayer', are not bypassed simply because other 'non traditional means of grace' are discovered. Robert Coles speaks of a young woman in one of the shanty towns of Rio de Janeiro. Each morning when she woke up she looked up at Ipanema, where the statue of the Christ towers over the city, and said 'Good morning' to Jesus. Each night before she went to sleep she would look up at the floodlit figure and say 'Good night' to Jesus. The woman said that the nuns had told her that Jesus looked particularly at the *favelistas*. 'Can you imagine,' they said, 'Jesus living in Copacabana, with a beautiful apartment, a fast boat and flashy cars like the rich people do?' 'The rich people don't own heaven,' she said, 'they cannot buy it even if they have millions of *cruzeiros*. God came to us as a poor man. He knows we would live better in Copacabana, but he knows that we have two lives – now, and the life to come. I am sure that God would like us to be rich, but he doesn't sit around, or call us to wait for miracles. He came to be with us, and that is a miracle in itself.'[5]

Once again the poor as 'moral agent', reflecting the antithesis of materialism, offers a perspective not only on the 'word' as Scripture, but the 'Word made flesh' that St John reveals as the Christ who 'lived among us'[6] - 'the miracle in itself'. Like most Western Christians, I live far from the margins of life. In my 'head' I can be converted to the understanding of the way the 'means of grace' appears in relation to the poor, but there is a deep resistance to appropriating the truth of the gospel that is revealed by these 'non traditional means of grace'. I have had to approach what has become known as 'the gospel option for the poor' through sacrament and prayer, rather than through appropriation of the 'word' within my deepest being. What I mean is this: that I've 'heard' what the 'word' says about a life oriented towards the poor, but so far I have been unable to appropriate it. My neighbouring vicar and old sparring partner, Canon David Galilee, once said as he jokingly introduced me: 'The higher Peter has gone in the Church, the more concerned he has become for the poor!' At some level I have been able to grasp the gospel imperative in terms of prayer, but it has all too often been like the prayer attributed to St Augustine, 'Lord, make me pure – but not yet.' In terms of the sacrament, I have broken bread in some extraordinary places, and felt the transforming power of Christ among the poor, but my heart quickly returns to stone when I am back among my own securities. I sense this remains a radical area of conversion, yet to be experienced.

SACRAMENT – 'WHO HERE IS THE
BREAD OF LIFE?'

During the visit to the community of religious sisters in Dublin I
mentioned earlier, we were greeted by the women. They were
angry. Sure, we were late, but then my friend was always late! The
anger was misdirected, though we experienced the full force of it!
It transpired that the three nuns had that day been told that they
were to be excommunicated from their order because, as their
superiors put it, 'while you may be living a gospel lifestyle, you
are not living a religious one.' Their refusal to place the needs of
the religious life above the pressing needs of the community had
cost them their vocation.

Their home, a tiny flat in the heart of the derelict community,
was open to all. Always around the kitchen table sat neighbours,
friends, all seeking some sense of belonging, of place. Whenever a
sympathetic priest arrived there was eucharist, breaking of bread.
One night Pat had celebrated communion with those assembled.
As he reached the words in the prayer of consecration, 'In the
night he was betrayed . . . Jesus took bread,' Pat stopped. Looking
around the assembled group he asked, 'Who here has been
betrayed? Would you tell us about it?' For over half an hour,
stories of betrayal poured out around the table. The group then
paused, and reflected further – 'What does it feel like to be
betrayed? Who betrays us? Who else is betrayed?' Before pro-
ceeding with the mass, Pat observed, 'Now you know how it was
for Jesus, and Jesus knows how it is for you.'

In this encounter so many things emerged for me: the difficulty
for institutional religion of the challenge of a genuine gospel
lifestyle. Of course I was shocked at the attitude of the religious
superiors; couldn't they see, I asked myself, how dreadful their
judgement was? But – and this makes me shudder not a little –
isn't that precisely what Jesus meant in his condemnation of the
scribal class and other groups as 'blasphemers against the Holy
Spirit'[7] when they condemned his liberating acts of healing, deliv-
erance and restoration? Juan Luis Segundo has observed that 'the
blasphemy from bad apologetics will always be pardonable . . .

what is not pardonable is using theology to turn real human liberation into something odious. The real sin against the Holy Spirit is refusing to recognise, with "theological joy", some concrete liberation that is taking place before one's very eyes.'[8]

The institutional Church speaks of its longing for change and innovation, yet is stifled by the need to control, and its requirement for conformity. Despite their material deprivation, there is so often a liberation among the poor, and that very liberation provides not only the moral agent, but the non traditional means of grace that enables them to understand, almost intuitively, what Joan Chittister believes that contemporary Christianity needs to understand and appropriate:

> God wants our lives. God wants a new point of view from us. God wants us to want the will of God more than our own comfort and consolation. God wants us to pay attention to the poor. 'Let justice roll down like waters', the scripture reads. Give more than the minimum. Give everyone their human due. Give everyone God's will for them.[9]

It is the difficulty of doing this, the sheer immovability of institution, that prevents so much from changing. It is institutional religion's act of betrayal that so often leaves people wounded, excluded and empty.

Eucharist invites us to place in a concrete way the story of our lives alongside the story of the institution(!) of the Last Supper, to open up the possibility of real transformation. When on occasions I have reached such a sharing in more informal eucharists, the power of connection among the group has been almost overwhelming. At the end of one parish conference I was presiding at communion. At the offertory of the bread and wine, I paused and said, 'We call this the bread of life. Who here is the bread of life?' Most present reacted with surprise, almost as if the question should not be asked, except for one man, who had come to the event somewhat reluctantly. 'I am,' he said. 'I am the bread of life to my family; without me they would go hungry, and be homeless.'

This relative outsider had understood something profound – our story *does* connect with that of the Jesus story; and if sacrament is 'the outward and visible sign of an inward and spiritual grace', then here was true sacramental understanding; 'We are what we eat.' The sacrament of bread and wine, the Lord's Supper, eucharist or the mass – call it what we will – stands as a sign not only of connection with God in which we literally, and almost offensively, 'munch on Christ' (as the Greek text of John 6:54 literally puts it!). It is also where we accept our humanity, and the humanity of others. Jesus' invitation to 'eat my flesh and drink my blood' is at its most basic level the acceptance of the whole person, of Christ, *and* of our fellow human beings. Our traditional understanding of this 'means of grace' has made much of the acceptance of the whole person of Christ affirmed at the sharing of the bread and wine, but much less of the acceptance of our fellow human beings, with whom we share the benefit of God's love. The innovation of the sharing of the peace has become the occasion for much jolly handshaking, but little real reconciliation in the great divides of life.

Once again for me this traditional means of grace was given fresh insight at a meal I once shared among the street people of Bangalore in India. For over twenty-five years generations of poor, destitute and homeless people made their way into the city from the villages and towns of South India. Many had pitched up on a street corner near a local hospital. Here they struggled to make a home out of the fragments of city life, living in tents without water or sanitation, and frequently the targets of violence. Illness was rife, children got sick and died, and because the poor are no angels, fights too were commonplace. The majority of the residents were Hindu, of the *dalit* peoples, so-called 'untouchables', belonging as they did to the lowest caste in Indian society.

'DINING IN THE KINGDOM OF GOD'

Around the Hindu festival of lights, Diwali, I visited a group of these people in the company of Christians who had been working for some time to help the community organize itself to enable it to obtain basic rights of sanitation, health care and food vouchers for their children. The first triumph was to obtain a standpipe and a tap – running water. This simple utility meant that the neighbourhood could be registered as a 'house', and the other benefits became possible. Mutual respect and love existed between the Christians and Hindus, and on the night of the festival we were invited to the ramshackle community of tents to share a feast.

Our arrival was greeted in the darkened street by firecrackers. Around the tent tables and chairs had been found, places of honour set up for the principal of the local seminary and myself. With great joy our hosts shared the food they had prepared. There was much laughter, though from my point of view little real understanding of the language. Our hosts did not eat with us; they watched attentively, smiling, busying themselves around us to make sure we had enough. When we asked when they would eat, they replied, 'When you have gone – then we can talk about you!' Speeches were made, the meal was over, and in the mingling that followed many tears were shed amidst the laughter and embracing. It was like a taste of heaven, where the whole of humanity has come together: those regarded as untouchable were being touched, those whose history had been one of exclusion, were being inclusive and included.

As we left the feast and walked up the darkened street, we began to reflect together. We all knew the Bible stories, particularly the one where Jesus says, 'when you have a party, invite the poor, the crippled, the lame, the blind; then you will be blessed, for they have no means to repay you and so you will be repaid when the upright rise again.'[10] Here was a paradox indeed, for it was those who were poor who had invited us! (For the sake of accuracy, I should say that the principal of the college had, at Christmas, provided food and gifts for the community.) But for me, at least, the point was made.

What always moves me in such circumstances is that so much that is grace-full happens. Our hosts told us they felt honoured by our coming; if only they knew how much we were honoured by their invitation! The touching, the holding, were symbolic and powerful too. For them we represented those who had historically excluded and defined them as 'untouchable'. Yet they accepted us, and we were given the privilege of shaking hands and embracing the 'little ones', the 'least' that Jesus so often speaks of.

Later I described this event as like 'dining in the kingdom of God'. And I so nearly missed it! Earlier that day I had been sick; I had been tired by a cold overnight journey, and I was tempted to settle for a more beguiling offer of a simple supper and an early bed! I wrote at the time, 'I'm glad that I didn't make excuses. It would have been to have been excluded myself; like the wedding guest who turned up without the garment! To make excuses is to exclude the possibility of heaven.' None of those who invited us were Christian, and yet the language and experience of the kingdom of heaven were happening all around us: the open-handed hospitality, the breaking down of the barriers that divide, the common search and longing for justice that include, all these were present, encapsulated in a few moments of history, yet providing real ground for hope.

That night I wrote: 'I understand tonight what Jesus meant when he said, "I have food to eat that you do not know about." '[11] There is a tendency to see Jesus' judgements about people not being able 'to enter the kingdom of heaven' as harsh, critical even. Possibly they are, but increasingly I see them as statements of regret at the joy that is missed by our refusal, reluctance, and inability to change our perspective and to see God's concrete acts.

It would be possible to debate endlessly whether this shared meal on the Bangalore street corner was eucharistic. What *kairos* moments like these expose is the poverty of such debate. Here were all the elements, broken bread, wine outpoured, justice sought, barriers broken, people reconciled, joy, celebration and thanksgiving, and for the record – scriptural reflection! Somehow, too, such an event presages images of the eschatological banquet. Was this what Jesus had in mind when at his own Last Supper he tells his hearers, 'From now on, I tell you, I shall never again drink wine until the day I drink the new wine with you in the kingdom of my Father'?[12]

PRAYER – 'ISN'T GOD OUR FATHER, ISN'T MARY OUR MOTHER?'

Recovering from my heart bypass operation, I found myself facing weariness and frustration at not being able to get back up to speed as fast as I wanted to. Various friends and acquaintances asked, 'What did you expect?' 'I didn't expect this to happen to me', was my often less than gracious response! I had been touched and moved by the prayers and good wishes of so many, but as so often it was an encounter of my friend Pat Clarke that put things into perspective for me. He had written from Brazil with a story that challenged all my preconceptions about spirituality, healing and courage.

'I will ask our people to pray,' he wrote. 'I always tell them there is great power in prayer, because it comes from so much faith. In fact, on Sunday, under yet another bridge here, I was talking to a woman after we had said the rosary, and she was telling me that she had just arrived from Paraiba in the North-east to visit her daughter, who had been knocked down and badly injured by a lorry. Her nine-month-old child had been killed outright. She herself and her grandchild had taken thirteen days to come. "Why so long?" I asked. "We depended on lifts." "Oh!" I said, "and what about food?" "We asked along the way. Ate when we got something, didn't eat when we got nothing." "And sleep," I asked. "On the side of the road, in hedges and fields, petrol stations and shop doors." I could only look at her in amazement. Then I said, "How did you go through all that hardship?" She looked up at the ceiling (which in fact was the underside of a concrete bridge) and replied, with her two arms extended, "Isn't God our Father? And isn't Mary our Mother?"'

Pat remarked, 'What can anyone say to that, Peter? I was reduced again to silence – to a profound reflection on my own ignorance and my ever so fragile faith: my habit of neatly circumventing the risks of a more authentically committed simplicity. Thank God for those apostles, prophets, pilgrims, anonymous angels of hope hidden away under bridges, unknown and rejected by the symbols of progress that roar by them triumphantly all day . . .'

Reflecting on my experience of Junkin's 'non traditional means of grace', on 'word', 'sacrament' and 'prayer', it seems that there is a graced-ness about the poor which makes them open to insights and values that cause those of us cluttered with sophistication to pause and think again about what really matters. Like Pat Clarke, I know how easy it is to 'neatly circumvent the risks of a more authentically committed simplicity.' Prayer that relies upon God in the kind of extremis experienced by the woman Pat encountered that day has always left me open-mouthed. There is about it a simplicity and an integrity, both of which expose the emptiness of much so-called faith in our own context, and the challenge to rediscover God who is the provider of all human need. As Daniel Berrigan has observed, 'God is the God, not of the big achievers and puny believers, but of the helpless, the victimized, and the distressed.'

I have frequently found myself asking, how can the poor be blessed, as Jesus is recorded as saying in St Luke's Gospel: 'How blessed are you who are poor: the kingdom of God is yours.'[13] Jesus implies that God's kingdom is a possession that already exists for the poor, whereas the rest of us have to enter it somehow. There is only part truth here, just as there is in allowing Jesus' other statement, 'the poor you will always have with you', to justify the continued exclusion of the poor. It seems to me that the poor are 'blessed' because the perceptions and possession of truth that they have, in part at least, come from their closeness to the stark realities of life. This gives them a certain graced-ness to see what really matters, and thus to perceive more clearly the priorities of God.

'TO RECEIVE GOD'S JUSTICE IS TO RECEIVE ACCESS TO A HOME'

What the poor have the right to expect from the world in which they live is that in it they will be offered a redemption from that which dehumanizes, and leaves them without hope. I have found

Robert Frost's poem 'Death of a Hired Man' offers something of a parable on this expectation. Frost pictures the hired man in conversation about where he belongs:

> 'Home', he mocked gently.
>   'Yes, what else but home?'
> It all depends on what you mean by home . . .
>
> 'Home is the place where, when you have to go there,
> they have to take you in.'
>
> 'I should have called it
> Something you somehow haven't to deserve.'[14]

It is this sense of 'something you somehow haven't to deserve' that lies at the heart of the gospel option for the poor. Reflecting on all of this some years ago, I found Wayne Meeks' remark, 'To receive God's justice is to receive access to a home',[15] helpful in understanding the challenge for the developed world, and in particular for the Christian community in facing the need to end poverty. God's justice, as we observed earlier, holds within it the idea that without the 'other' – be it God or neighbour – we cannot be complete. Meeks puts his idea into the domestic context of home:

> Home is where everyone knows your name. Home is where you can always count on being confronted, forgiven, loved and cared for. Home is where there is always a place for you at the table. And, finally, home is where you can count on sharing what is on the table . . . According to the creation narratives, not just human beings, but every one of God's creatures has a right to a name and access to "table".[16]

Meeks does not have in mind here some middle-class concept of home. He is speaking prophetically about what belonging to the community of creation means, where people are known, valued and recognized as needing confrontation, forgiveness, love and care; and where there is enough for all at the 'table' of earth's fecundity and where gratitude becomes true eucharist.

The late Guillermo 'Bill' Cook, who did so much to inspire so many people for the task of the Church to meet the expectation of the poor, shared with us a story which for me sums up the endplay of the *undersong* of the poor:

'We are sitting round a very large table. It has an enormous cloth on it. There is one empty seat, which we are keeping for the "Unseen Guest". The table is groaning from all the good things to eat and drink from the produce of the whole world. We're having a good time. Mostly we are unaware that under the table there is movement – people hidden, save for the occasional hand. They have no food; all they get are any scraps that fall on to the floor. People are scrabbling about for anything that might come. Occasionally they touch our feet. Some of us just kick. Others pass the occasional plateful down. Sometimes people move up to the table, and others move under it. But they are way over the other side of the table, and we scarcely notice. We are afraid of the tables being turned, so we don't pay too much attention.

'Then suddenly Jesus comes into the room. We're pleased to see him – we offer him the empty chair, but he ignores us, and lifting up the edge of the tablecloth he crawls under the table. Around us people are saying, "He can't be the real Christ . . . he is a false Christ – anti-Christ." Nevertheless some say, "What's he doing down there?" Soon we hear laughter, singing, freedom songs; and then the tablecloth lifts, and Jesus leads a little child, then a procession of children, women and men from under the table; and they form a large circle round the table. Silence has fallen. It is clear something has to happen. We look at the table; then at the people excluded from it.

'Then someone from Japan, or somewhere that people sit on the floor to eat food, suggests that if we shortened the legs of the table and stretched out the cloth, there would be room for all around the table; and it is obvious there is plenty to eat and drink. We know the choice exists for us: to ignore what has happened or to go and sit down there nearer the floor.'

As a parable, it depicts the dilemma for those of us who, like me, prefer their religion consolatory and private, rather than demanding the public commitment to changing the inequity of our world, where 'God disappears from the heart' to one where God is over all and in all, and where justice and righteousness dwell. Before Bill told this story, he would often refer to a Garfield cartoon with the caption set below Garfield sitting with a knife and fork in his hand: 'Whenever life gets too complicated, I just sit down and wait for someone to bring me lunch.' In addressing in my journey the ongoing difficulty, not to say 'complication', of choosing the poor and working to end poverty, I think I am still 'waiting for lunch'. But I have learned not to despair and, as in some mysterious way the movement of the butterfly's wings in the desert shakes the whole universe, so does the simplest action on behalf of the poor. After all, Jesus said it only has to be 'giving a cup of water in my name'. Just so long as we do not allow ourselves to be beguiled into believing that is all that needs to change.

I have spoken so much in this chapter of my friend Pat Clarke – the 'auld guru' and my angel, as I sometimes call him – that I must close with an Irish blessing bestowed on me at one of our meetings. It somehow sums up the *undersong:*

> I saw a stranger yester-een.
> I put food in the eating place,
> Drink in the drinking place,
> Music in the listening place,
> And in the blessed name of the Triune,
> He blessed myself and my house,
> My cattle and my dear ones,
> And the lark said in his song
> Often, often, often,
> Goes the Christ in the stranger's guise.

7

THE UNDERSONG
OF PRAYER

'NO BATHING' SAID THE SIGNS around the site of a holy well.
At the same time there were changing facilities for pilgrims to
take the waters. In the mud near the pool was a single footprint.
Some anonymous pilgrim had journeyed from who knows where
to seek God. The footprint was an eloquent and moving testimony to humanity's ceaseless longing for God. Such simple signs
of searching often move me, and have frequently been the means
by which I have learned to pray a bit more, and possibly a little
better. Prayer is the constant footprint in the mud or, as Moses
discovered, the naked foot on the holy ground of God's creation.
Prayer is the first step, and the constant step of the pilgrim
journey. 'Pilgrim ... there are no paths ... paths are made by
walking', I read somewhere once, and it takes prayer to walk
straight on the pilgrim path.

It was on one of my many pilgrimages that I met the person
who most influenced my thought about prayer, and my praying.
I was in the bookshop of Chicago's O'Hare airport when I
discovered a remarkable journal, *An Interrupted Life* by a Dutch
Jewess, Etty Hillesum.[1] Etty died in Auschwitz, but her legacy of
understanding of the human condition, the nature of God and her
insights into prayer, lives on. Besides struggling with the awful
realities of imminent arrest and deportation, she struggled with
the things in life that concern us all: fears, hopes, unrequited
longing, her own sensuality, her passionate concern for others,
and much else besides. A deeply tactile person, she was also

profoundly spiritual and had a longing for God and an intimacy of relationship that I have only begun to glimpse. She was not a conventional believer. Her belief in Jesus Christ was not accompanied by adherence to the Christian faith, neither was her Jewishness determined by her observance of Judaism.

'There is a deep well inside me,' she wrote, 'and in it dwells God. I am there too. But more often than not stones and silt block the well and God is buried beneath – then he must be dug out again.' I find it easy to identify with this insight. Within us all there is a 'deep well', and within it lie both God and our deepest self. When, to use Etty's imagery, we allow God to be 'dug out', we also discover something of our true selves. In the *undersong* of prayer there are moments when the 'stones and silt' that 'block the well' get removed, often in the most unlikely of times and places. Etty's experiences of God's revelation and her own deepening insights into herself, as well as those around her, came against the backdrop of the most mind-numbing horrors. My own experiences of God's revelation have frequently occurred in the presence of those who suffer.

In the week following the Real IRA bomb that blew up my wife's home town of Omagh, in Northern Ireland, in which twenty-nine people died and over two hundred were horrifically injured, we returned, as I have already mentioned, for the Memorial Service. Standing on the steps of the town hall with many of those who had been bereaved, we talked with one man who had been widowed. 'I do not bother God much, apart from mass on Sundays,' he said. 'I was dreading the moment when my wife's coffin was to be lowered into the ground. But as it was, I was filled with an enormous sense of inner strength, which did not come from me.' Explaining such experiences is not easy, nor always appropriate, but in the *undersong*, that 'yearning which is both . . . the pull and push of the journey', we discover that what has been sustained in the ordinary – for this man mass on Sundays – is exposed in the extraordinary, and God is 'dug out' or, perhaps slightly more prosaically, God is freed to be God.

Moments like these expose a holy longing. It is a longing that exists in what Etty Hillesum has called a 'vast loneliness'. When somehow we glimpse that there is no space free from God's presence, then our 'loneliness' and the 'longing' can be met. I know few people who do not at some time or another admit to either the desire to pray or the practice of prayer, though they do not necessarily see themselves as 'religious' in any formal sense. It is as if there are times when the 'really deep well inside' yearns for the unblocking of the 'stones and silt', and God somehow *must* be released.

TO WHAT KIND OF GOD
DO WE PRAY?

For many, the question is, to what kind of God do we pray? Etty's experience, and mine too, is of a God met, initially at least, at some moment of crisis, fear, despair, or awareness of unworthiness or sinfulness. My wife Dee, however, speaks of her first encounter with God as being wonderment as she stood aged three in the light of a sun-bathed stained glass window. These moments – whether of loneliness, longing or wonderment – can be those in which people discover that there is no space free of God. Discovering this truth in whatever way seems to be necessary within the human condition, the American poet and philosopher, Henry David Thoreau, once observed, 'The mass of men lead lives of quiet desperation.'[2] But he went on to say, 'We are constantly invited to be what we are . . .' Many people lead lives that are full of desperation, unable to lift their eyes above the daily grind to be or become what they are. All too many bear out the experience of a woman whose story I heard a while ago: 'You know my family is about a medical bill and a tax payment away from the street. My husband was laid off in August. We are just about stuck together with scotch tape and baling wire to look presentable.' And stories like hers I've heard a thousand times.

The God to whom we pray must in some way meet such needs, but we also need a God who takes us beyond ourselves. Dag Hammarskjøld, the former United Nations Secretary General, who met an untimely death in an air crash, recognized this and invited people 'to pray that your loneliness may spur you into finding something to live for, great enough to die for.'[3] Prayer, it seems to me, has to make it possible for those who 'are just about stuck together with scotch tape and baling wire' – whether as a result of the drudgery of life, the immediacy of loss, or dealing with the inexplicable – to find that 'something to live for, great enough to die for.' Or, as Thoreau has it, to respond to the invitation 'to be what we are'.

In order for people to respond to God, to become what they are, they need some confidence in who God is for them. The Scriptures constantly affirm God as loving and his people as beloved, though it has to be said that at times his Church has been more concerned with conveying a God who is angry, full of judgement and at best ambivalent about loving. I was brought up in a faith not dissimilar from the parody which Gerard Hughes also sees as many people's image of God:

> God was a family relative much admired by Mum and Dad, who described him as very loving, a great friend of the family and very interested in all of us. Eventually we are taken to visit 'Good Old Uncle George'. He lives in a formidable mansion, is bearded, gruff and threatening. We cannot share our parents' professed admiration for this jewel in the family. At the end of the visit, Uncle George turns to address us: 'Now listen, dears,' he begins, looking very severe, 'I want to see you here once a week – and if you fail to come, let me just show you what will happen to you.'[4]

Hughes then amusingly parodies a picture of hell which scares the life out of the children, and concludes with Mum and Dad saying on the way home: 'And now don't you love Uncle George with "all your heart and soul, mind and strength?" And we, loathing the monster, each say "Yes I do", because to say anything else would be to join the queue at the furnace.'

A GOD WHO HEARS THE CRIES
OF THE WRONGED

For many people there is a kind of religious schizophrenia about God, as Hughes observes. We are told of God's love, but so much happens in our world which seems to deny it that we are left with a question mark at least. Over the years I have struggled with this.

Like most people I have had difficulties with it but, like many others, I can bear testimony to moments of disclosure where God is revealed as loving, and I as beloved. My earliest recollection of this was in the back of my father's ancient car coming back from a pantomime presentation of *Peter Pan*. It had been brilliant. The stage show to my nine-year-old eyes had been quite magical, but something had happened after the show and my father had blamed me. I know what happened wasn't my fault, though I have long since forgotten the incident, but I went into a decline. I told him I had hated the show, I wished I hadn't come, that I wanted to be with my friends, not my ghastly family who were always allowing me to be picked on! Needless to say this did not go down well, and I was accused of ingratitude and selfishness! My grandmother, a devout and caring woman, was sitting beside me in the back of the car. She whispered, 'Think of Jesus.' I do not know now what I 'thought', but what I experienced was an extraordinary sense of what I can only call 'otherness', and in my desolation I found a calm, and the beginnings of a consolation that came from beyond myself.

Prayer is not about avoiding the realities which humanity experiences, but facing them and discovering God in the midst of tears and sadness. 'There is . . . a sign that is sovereign among the signs that humankind makes: the sign of tears. There is also a speech which is privileged and takes precedence over other speech, even speech in the words of scripture: the cries of the wronged'; and 'there is wrong done by words, and the cries of those wounded by words will be heard in Heaven, and God will take their side . . . for tears are the human speech God privileges above all others.'[5] And we know that so much of our world is marked by tears, the cries of the wronged, those wounded by words.

On the surface it is not easy to see how God hears the cries and takes the side of the wounded. And it would be naïve to believe that there are not difficulties in accepting such an understanding of God, or indeed paths in prayer, without at some level facing the more unpalatable realities of a God who at times appears to be totally powerless, or absent.

People like me have never had to face serious privation in the form of hunger, homelessness, or poverty, nor the possibility of arrest, torture, imprisonment or death for anything I am, or believe. Therefore it requires an enormous leap of imagination to stand alongside those for whom such experiences are an awesome daily reality. But Etty Hillesum and thousands of her compatriots faced years of anxiety, certain that one day there would be a knock at the door and they would be taken for liquidation solely on the grounds of their ethnic origin. At such a time Etty wrote:

> Dear God, these are anxious times. Tonight for the first time I lay in the dark with burning eyes, as scene after scene of human suffering passed before me. I shall promise You one thing, God, just one very small thing: I shall never burden my today with cares about my tomorrow, although that takes some practice. Each day is sufficient unto itself. I shall try to help You, God, to stop my strength ebbing away, though I cannot vouch for it in advance. But one thing is becoming increasingly clear to me: that You cannot help us, that we must help You to help ourselves. And that is all we can manage these days, and also all that really matters: that we safeguard that little piece of You, God, in ourselves. And perhaps in others as well. Alas, there doesn't seem to be much that You Yourself can do about our circumstances about our lives. Neither do I hold You responsible. You cannot help us, but we must help You and defend Your dwelling place in us to the last.

Few pieces of writing have made me question my all-too-easy 'fix it' faith as this passage. Nor have any words caused me to ask more questions about how to pray than these. On many occasions I have shared Etty's story in conferences and retreats, and nearly always I quote this insight. It always produces a thoughtful reaction. For some it is like a light being turned on, while for others, like me, there remains great difficulty in accepting the premise, 'You cannot help us, God.'

SAFEGUARDING GOD'S PRESENCE
WITHIN

Over the years I have thought long and hard about Etty's premise
that God cannot help us. I have had to unpack this remarkable
diary note. Etty's imagination, fuelled by the all-too-present
reality of unspeakable suffering, is depressingly the reality for
millions today. Etty's experience has nurtured in me a creative
imagination when seeking to pray about our suffering world,
and such imagining has prompted moments of engagement with
suffering people, whether it has been writing letters on behalf of
prisoners of conscience, walking the slums of cities around the
world, or finding my way into the presence of Tariq Aziz,
the Prime Minister of Iraq, to plead for compassion for Iraq's
people.

But it is Etty's reflection on her promise to God never to
'burden my today with cares about my tomorrow . . . Each day is
sufficient unto itself', that has caused me to look afresh at how I
deal with life's intransigencies. Here, Etty echoes Jesus' words,
'So do not worry about tomorrow: tomorrow will take care of
itself. Each day has enough trouble of its own.'[6] There is something profoundly true and liberating about such an attitude to life.
Most of the things we worry about we cannot change at that
particular moment. There is a time and place for such change, and
it is often tomorrow in some form. I have learned something of
that contemplation that does not 'burden my today with cares
about my tomorrow', though I agree with Etty that it does take
some practice. Part of that practice relies upon the imagination,
of putting oneself into the situation feared and addressing it from
the point of view of the desired outcome. This is not to ignore the
difficulties, but to put the situation in its best light before
commending the resolution to God.

The idea of us 'helping God', as Etty suggests she must do, is
not unfamiliar in Christian prayer, but is an approach that is often
neglected, particularly in church, in favour of intercessions where
the buck gets passed to God to sort things out! Etty sees 'helping
God' as safeguarding 'that little piece of You, God, in ourselves.

And perhaps in others as well.' This, too, resonates with traditions in spirituality that are concerned with nurturing the presence of God. Nurturing, as those who have to do with children know, takes time, patience and understanding. Activists like me tend to have to learn the way of solitude and reflection, that essential inward 'alone-ness', in order to let the 'silt and stones that block the well' of access to God be released. It, too, takes practice. Jesus, in commending patterns of prayer, encouraged: 'when you pray, go to your private room, shut yourself in, and so pray to your Father who is in that secret place; and your Father who sees all that is done in secret will reward you.'[7]

What remains tricky is the idea that 'You [God] cannot help us.' This is a bleak scenario. Because nothing in my experience touches anything like the humiliation, dehumanization and self-disgust imposed upon people like Etty, I am cautious about dismissing it altogether. A window into understanding lies for me in Hillesum's insight, 'we must help You defend Your dwelling place in us to the last.' Without the dwelling place of God within us – the 'well', if you like – human beings lose their humanity. For that which makes us human is the image and likeness of God. When humanity is so dehumanized that the very possibility of this God-like identity being lost seems possible, despair follows. I believe that, like Job, Etty wrote from a place of despair.

Those who have experienced such places of despair must be listened to in silence and reverence. If we are to find ways of praying that do not violate their experience, we must listen to their insights. When John McCarthy and Brian Keenan, held hostage in Beirut, were released, Keenan reflected, 'For us who have been in that angel fearful place, there remain things of which we cannot speak.' Another former hostage, Jean Paul Kauffman, observed, 'the long bloody night remained too heavy a night to be transmitted to those who had not experienced it. This incurable wound, which we former hostages carry still, seems to me incommunicable. One day perhaps . . . I will feel like a diver who slowly comes to the surface.' When people break the surface after times of privation, experiences of God are often reflected upon, where God is both 'absent' and 'present'.

PRAYING TO GOD WHO IS ABSENT, PRESENT, AND REVEALED

Within both Jewish and Christian tradition there lies a little-known element in the *undersong* of prayer. It is that of the absence of God, *deus absconditus*. Throughout her diaries Etty Hillesum dialogued with God, believing God present, even if hidden. The psalms frequently reflect the sense of God's hiddenness, or abandonment. Cries such as 'you have abandoned and humiliated us ... You hand us over like sheep for slaughter ... Why are you asleep?'[8] somehow wake us up and take us away from cosy, easy answers. To accuse God is a courageous act, but often it is a more honest reaction than to praise God when there is little sign of glory. But, as so often with our attempts at understanding God, we find other traditions within our faith that lead us to finding God in the most unlikely of places. God's presence, his *shekinah*, or glory, is often revealed in the Scriptures as being among his people in slavery or exile; and the cry of God, 'in distress I am at his side',[9] litters the Bible from Egypt to Babylon.

I have particularly appreciated those who have sought to create a synthesis of the traditions of God as absent, and of God as present, by espousing the idea that the hidden face of God is somehow 'compatible with God's existence' and that there is 'actual presence within his silence'.[10] The example is trivial, I know, but how often in recent years I have sat in a room with a loved one in total silence for a long time. The absence of communication has not negated the presence within the silence, though each of us is privy to the activity of our own hearts.

These brave insights into God each in their own way help to discern in prayer's *undersong* a richness of understanding concerning the nature of God, and a profound challenge as to how to make the prayer of intercession one that releases and exposes God in his world. And if I am to find an answer to Etty's haunting words 'You cannot help us', it is in some way to reflect on the wider understandings of God held by people in all kinds of circumstances.

The prayer of intercession is the most costly of prayers. It is prayer that offers hope for our world. To *intercede* is to stand between parties in conflict or tension, and somehow to hold the tension and seek a resolution, an ending of the causes of the conflict or tension. As a social and political activist, I have learned something of the task of intercession in the search for justice, whether for prisoners of conscience, racial awareness, nuclear disarmament, reconciliation in Ireland, or peace in the Middle East. Prayer as intercession is undertaking this task on behalf of others for the sake of God's wider purposes of restoring peace and wholeness to fractured humanity.

But it is not easy to bear such responsibility, neither is it easy to pray in this way. 'We are not easily reduced to prayer. We who grope towards praying today are like a city gutted by fire. The struggle against injustice has exacted from us an awful cost', observes Walter Wink.[11] I agree with this, because the struggle against injustice is so hard and unremitting. It is hard, too, because prayer has become such an intensely private act, something it is not meant to be. Christian activists are remarkably reluctant to pray, at least publicly, yet it is as much a part of the struggle as any protest, demonstration or positive action.

There is, of course, private prayer to be prayed. It is the prayer that faces the anger and compulsions that drive us all, 'that interior battlefield where the decisive victory must be won before any engagement in the outer world is even possible.'[12] The prayer of intercession must be accompanied by the 'private' act of dealing with the inner demons of fear, anger, despair and the desire to transfer all on to God. To enter into the task of intercession requires a spirit of hope, courage and defiance.

PRAYER . . . 'IS BELIEVING THE FUTURE INTO BEING'

'Intercession,' says Wink, 'is spiritual defiance of what is, in the name of what God has promised. Intercession visualizes a future to the one apparently fated by the momentum of contradictory forces. It breathes the air of a time yet to be into the suffocating atmosphere of present reality. The message is clear: History belongs to the intercessors, who believe the future into being.' We all know that history, too, is made by people with ideas, visions, dreams. All too often those visions and dreams involve self-aggrandizement, the misuse of power, and the subjugation and enslavement of others. But in a sense history makers are inter-cessors, standing between what is and what might be, bringing them together in a new kind of future. The issue for people of faith is, can we become the new history makers, envisioning in our prayers and lifestyle the possibility at the heart of Christian prayer: 'Your kingdom come on earth'?

In the *undersong* of prayer I have wrestled with this possibility. During some days with my friend Walter Wink we discussed Etty Hillesum's challenge and found ourselves deeply respectful of her conclusions in the midst of her awful reality. At the same time, Wink moved the argument on, providing a useful synthesis, which has enabled intercessory prayer for me to have both an integrity and hope. Wink speaks of intercession as 'Hope that envisions the future and then acts as if the future is then irresistible, thus helping to create the reality for which it longs', and of God depending on the intercessions of those who care enough to shape the earth more humanly than it is. For most of us the question is, do we care enough? I ask this not to judge, except myself, but because of the ease with which we slip into the idea that handing things over to God, or drawing things to God's attention, is the limit of our responsibility!

Intercessory prayer is a co-creative activity: it involves those who care enough to shape the world differently with a God whose power is, in some measure at least, released by such human longing and participation. It is a recognition that in silence, as well as presence, God initiates prayer; for from the raw material of human privation rises the voice of liberation, and it becomes possible to observe that God's power, rather than ours, answers the world's needs. During a visit to El Salvador in 1988 I met with the Lutheran Bishop Medardo Gomez. Traditionally Lutherans in the El Salvadoran Church do not have bishops. Gomez explained his elevation to the episcopate with wry amusement. For a number of years he had faced daily threats, intimidation and summary arrest, leading to periods of imprisonment and torture, for his opposition to the brutality of the government and its death squads. His congregation reasoned that if he were to be made a bishop his arrests might be fewer! Shortly after our visit, Gomez was once again arrested. Messages were sent from his church to pray and to intercede on his behalf. I wrote a letter outlining the situation to the *Independent* newspaper in London. Various clergy phoned me telling me that they had used my letter as the focus for their intercessions that day. Shortly afterwards a message came from El Salvador advising of Gomez' release. His captors, who had intended to kill him, told him, 'You have many friends in the world, otherwise you would be dead.' I tell this story because it seems to me to encapsulate the nature of intercession as co-creative activity with God. To cry, to pray and work for justice remains an imperative of intercessory activity.

PRAYER AND THE VICTIMHOOD OF OUR PASSIONS

Intercession of this order requires space to deal with what someone has called the 'victimhood of our passions'. There is a need within ourselves to deal with our obsessions, angers, and despair, as well as our more secret sins. But our confession cannot stop there. It needs to include a recognition, not only of how hard the struggle is, and how powerful the forces of evil are that are at work in our world, but also that we have a vision of God that is big enough to lead us into hope, and to discover a God who can help us. The vision of this new order includes the concept of partnership, interdependence, equality of opportunity and mutual respect, which is able to cut across all distinctions and divisions. This 'egalitarian realm', as Wink puts it, is one that 'repudiates violence, domination hierarchies, patriarchy, racism and authoritarianism.'[13] Jesus described such a vision as the reign of God, 'the kingdom of heaven'.

Dealing with the victimhood of our passions, and truly desiring the reign of God to break in on the human story, does not come without cost. Today a great deal is said about 'apologizing' for actions committed in the past, from slavery to apartheid in South Africa. I believe there would be much to be gained from a universal application of the principle of both 'apology' and 'reparation' at some level. How it should be organized is not within my ken, but I sense that within the Church at least we need to rediscover a mode of confession that takes us from the purely personal into this more communal, international sphere of both seeking forgiveness and practising it.

Fiona Shaw, who is one of the English National Theatre's leading actresses, spoke of a visit to a closed order of nuns. A woman of faith, Shaw was to some extent returning to her roots. She confessed that at the beginning of her stay she observed the rituals of the nuns with an amused eye. The practice of confessing sin by silently prostrating oneself before the abbess seemed to Shaw in the early hours of her stay humiliating and not a little absurd. As the days went by, she came to reflect that there was something deeply moving and powerful about this act. She concluded that if, perhaps, all of us could take time to confess our sinfulness through a gesture, the world might be a better place.

Besides the act of prostration, which Shaw described as 'a consummate act of penitence', the nuns practised other acts of personal penitence by kneeling, wherever happened to be the point of recall. She observed one nun with a sudden, mischievous smile on her face, a few moments later kneel and presumably confess. 'I would love,' remarked Fiona Shaw, 'to have known what prompted such a delicious smile followed by a penitent act!'

What Shaw observed in her reflection about the gesture and the prostration of confession is not insignificant for both our personal life, and that of nations. There is a need for prayer to move beyond the personal and pietistic into the gestures of penitence and prostration in the wider world. Perhaps nations like China and Japan – and others which have been both victim and oppressor – can find gestures to acknowledge their mutual penitence. Or the Western powers, whose 'sins' of exploitation and human violation began in colonizing eras and continue today in the aggression of the market, also require some kind of prostration before the court of humanity. The Jubilee 2000 and Drop the Debt campaigns could provide such a gesture.

PRAYER AS AFFIRMING THAT 'LIFE IS BEAUTIFUL'

There has to be a way of dealing with what Etty Hillesum calls 'a cosmic sadness'. In her diaries she reflects on a conversation with a friend, Ilse Blumenthal:

> Yes, life is beautiful and I value it anew at the end of every day, even though I know that the sons of mothers . . . are being murdered in concentration camps. And you must be able to bear your sorrow – even if it seems to crush you, you will be able to stand up again, for human beings are so strong, and your sorrow must become an integral part of yourself, part of your body and soul, and you mustn't run away from it, but bear it as an adult. Do not relieve your feelings through hatred; do not seek to be avenged . . . Give your sorrow all the space and shelter in yourself that is its due, for if everyone bears his grief honestly and courageously, the sorrows of this world will abate. But if you cannot clear a decent shelter for your sorrow, and instead reserve a place inside you for hatred and thoughts of revenge, from which sorrows will be born for others, then sorrows will never cease in this world, and will multiply. And if you have given sorrow the space its gentle origins demand, then you may truly say: life is beautiful and rich – so beautiful and rich that it makes you want to believe in God.[14]

Prayer that does not acknowledge at its heart that all of God's creatures have a right to say out of their own experience 'life is beautiful and rich' is not truly prayer. But such a comprehension of prayer is only possible if we hold a vision for the possibility of a new society – an 'egalitarian realm', if you like – or the reign of God 'on earth as it is in heaven'. Shortly after the Sandinista victory in Nicaragua in the 1980s, I visited the country. Like many, I had been inspired by these champions of the underclass taking on the might of the ruling families, and winning. Of course, much was not as it seemed at the time, and the psalmist's injunction, 'Do not put your trust in princes, in any child of Adam, who has no power to save',[15] should have been better heeded. But there were remarkable moments, and Father Ernesto Cardenal was a major influence for good. One Saturday morning I met him in the room in the palace of the former President Samoza, where Samoza had personally tortured Tomas Borge.[16] Borge gained something of a reputation for his magnanimous act of forgiveness of his jailers and torturers, whose release and safety he ensured when the Sandinistas came to victory.

Cardenal spoke to us that morning about seeking to bring about structures that produced justice, freedom from fear for all, and the renewal of culture where music, art, poetry, books, and films could all contribute to the renewal of society. It was a dream for a new order, still to be fulfilled in Nicaragua and, indeed, throughout the world! Political movements, particularly revolutionary or fascist ones, have often driven out the beautiful, the creative arts, or tried to harness them for propaganda purposes. My all-too-uncritical embrace of the Nicaraguan revolution taught me many things. I learned to see the danger of embracing human liberation brought about through revolution as God's liberation. I have no doubt that there was something of God's liberating activity within what happened, but God's justice can only be discerned when humanity is freed of all that oppresses. Likewise, it is important to discern that God acts within human institutions, but not exclusively so, and that the discernment of beauty in culture and music, are only glimpses of the beauty of God.

My encounter with Cardenal was accompanied by reading Gerry Hughes' travelogue, *In Search of a Way*.[17] He reflected, 'Whatever form the new society may take, it must not destroy our ability to appreciate what is beautiful. There is something very wrong in such dedication to the ideals of social justice that we can no longer enjoy beautiful things for their own sake.' There is an important truth here. In my journeyings I have often witnessed the struggle for justice being waged in situations of great poverty, but frequently set in, or in sight of, places of great beauty. The silent witness of God who desires our good and our joy is present in that which is beautiful and leads us ultimately to worship. Intercessory prayer takes us not only into co-creativity with God, but into a place of worship that God's essence is beauty, splendour to be worshipped and adored.

In the *undersong* of prayer the act of adoration – of worship – needs to take us beyond ourselves, beyond the footprint in the mud, even beyond our co-creativity with God, into the realm of the worship of God, who creates all that is beautiful and lovely. It is the discovery of God for who God is, rather than for what I, or any of us, need God to be. When this happens we enter into the possibility of what Rilke has called 'serenity'. Looking at Rodin's sculptures, Rilke said, 'I must learn not his art, but his deep inner serenity, for the sake of creation.'[18] Finding what Christians often call 'the peace of God' is discovering God's 'deep inner serenity'. For whether or not God is present, absent or hidden, whether God can help us or not, what matters is that God is discerned 'for the sake of creation' and that we, like Hillesum, must 'defend God's dwelling place in us to the last.'

And prayer in the end must open for us the vision of what is to be. 'Look,' says the Book of Revelation, 'here God lives among human beings. He will make his home among them; they will be his people . . . He will wipe away all tears from their eyes; there will be no more death, and no more mourning or sadness or pain. The world of the past has gone.'[19] Once or twice in life the privilege is given to glimpse a vision of what is to be.

On 9 May 1999 a mixed bag of humanity stood in the vandalized Anglican Church of St George in Baghdad, and we celebrated eucharist. Gathered around the restored altar were some twenty people: Christians – Catholics, Anglicans, Aramaic – and others, including Muslims and those apparently with no faith, people sent to 'mind' us. It was both profound and moving: the UN Humanitarian Director, Hans Von Sponeck, exchanging the peace with an Iraqi government commissar; a Muslim seeking a blessing at the administration of the communion; Catholics, Protestants and Orthodox sharing bread and wine together. So many miracles! A vision of the kingdom to come! Here, too, the *undersong* of prayer was played in reconciliation, as German wept in the presence of Briton and together they grieved the pain of division and war beneath the chipped war memorials. Here, too, Etty's 'stones and silt' were removed in the symbolic uniting of enemies and friends, Semite and Caucasian.

Somehow, in those few moments, we experienced eucharist as the ultimate act of prayer. Here were individuals, and yet a group. Here was prayer, private and corporate, intercessory and contemplative. In the breaking of bread and the taking, or in the sharing of the peace, many diversities were reconciled in a cosmic moment of transcendent unity. Here in a single moment all humanity was gathered into the eternal self-giving of the Father and the Son, by the grace of the Spirit. Somehow the *undersong* of cosmic connection was made. As Vaclav Havel has discerned it, 'by perceiving ourselves as part of the river, we take responsibility for the river as a whole.'

8

THE UNDERSONG
OF SUFFERING

I WAS TRAVELLING WITH A COLLEAGUE who is a philosopher.
Our journey took several hours and was interrupted by stopping
for dinner on the way. It was one of those 'time beyond time'
experiences when the conversation that flowed was both stimulating and life giving, as well as being quite deep. This particular
individual is one of those men who can genuinely be described
as 'good'. He has enormous insight, profound compassion, is
unfailingly courteous and is both interesting and interested in all
that happens around him. As our journey drew to its close I
ventured to say, 'You are one of the most Christian people
I know, in the sense that your way of life, and your love and
compassion, together with your deep concern for others is
exemplary, and yet you do not profess to be a believer.' 'No,' he
replied after a few moments of reflection, 'I cannot believe in
God for two reasons: first because of undeserved suffering, and
second because I could not accept God as being omnipotent.'

Despite the lateness of the hour we continued our discussion
for some time, and picked up our conversation again the following morning. Of course it would be easy to say that many of
the explanations that he had received on the problem of suffering
were inadequate and ill-formed, but in a way that is true for
any argument that seeks to deal with the profound mystery of
suffering. Suffering is part of the *undersong* of all our journeys in
one way or another. While there are times when we can see
particular forms of suffering as the consequence of events, or

circumstances, nevertheless for most of us it remains a mystery, particularly when we face suffering in what we might describe as undeserved ways.

As a priest I have had to face my share of situations in which people have experienced 'undeserved suffering', often through the untimely death of loved ones, or the contracting of so far incurable illnesses. Every time an occasion arises where such suffering has to be faced, I too am faced with the questions about the meaning of suffering and the omnipotence of God. Looking into the eyes of someone who seeks comfort, an explanation, some straw to grasp, always promotes in me a sense of impotence and questioning.

One morning a close friend rang. 'Patrick is dead,' he blurted out. Patrick was the nine-month-old son, a lively, apparently healthy child, who in the night had died a 'cot death'. A few days later to a packed church I offered some reflections. They did not come easily. I spoke of his little life, and of how people had described Patrick. I told of how through his 'nosiness' and 'smiles' he had brought people together. Saying it, I hoped it would not appear banal. I said, too, that he had brought us in some way to God, and that like God we had shown compassion, love, and generosity towards the grieving family. I reminded folk that Patrick's innocence had made us aware of our own lost innocence, and that in some small way he had helped us to start again in our relationships with one another. Saying this too, I feared being thought preachy.

Much of this was a prelude for trying to say something that enabled us as a group of people to enter into the awful mystery of loss, and somehow to find God there. I reflected that God does not will or cause suffering, but that God, like us, knows about and experiences suffering. I said, too, that God knows how we feel when the mystery of suffering and death touch our lives. I reminded them of Jesus as one who has borne our griefs and carried our sorrows. I risked quoting the psalm writer who said, 'My help comes from the Lord'.[1] Not my pain, my tragedy, my grief – but my help.

What seemed to touch a chord was the reflection that God is supporting us. I said that I believed there were certain things that

God did not control. This, however, does not prevent God being God, but reveals the possibility that God is being God by helping us to bear the grief and the pain we experience. I suggested that being angry at what happened was OK too, but that we did not have to be mad at God, though I suggested if we needed to be angry, God could handle it. We can recognize our anger at life's unfairness, acknowledge our instinctive compassion at people's suffering, and see it as coming from God who teaches us to be angry at injustice, and to feel compassion. Instead of feeling our anger as opposed to God, we can know that our indignation is God's indignation too at the unfairness. Simply, when we cry out in grief and anger, God does too, and he is on our side, as we are on his.

SUFFERING CHANGES OUR PERCEPTION OF GOD

In the *undersong* of suffering, discovering who God is for us may well change our perception. Trying to discern whether God is all-powerful or not is a philosophical and theological discussion that has spanned the centuries. Faced with the immediacy of pain and grief, it is possible to reflect with integrity that God does not control all things at all times; and that God too faces pain, anger and a longing for the end of misery.

Faith is about relationship with God, discerning what God is like, and how God can be offered our allegiance, service, and ultimately our adoration and worship. That is seldom easy, and our faith is often tempered with doubts and questions. However, I believe we come closest to God, and to some under-standing of suffering, when we discern in ourselves those elements of compassion, of grief, even of anger at the unfairness of it all. Here we are in a real sense entering into God, and finding God for who God is. This is not to say that the mystery is not a deep one. One sermon at the memorial of one little child does not give us either an adequate answer to the mystery of suffering, nor a complete picture of the nature of God.

Occasionally, however, someone's suffering, though tragic in itself, can offer real inspiration, hope and renewal of faith. On

Good Friday a year or so ago I was called to our local hospice and asked if I would baptize and confirm a young woman of eighteen who was not expected to live long. Her name was Salomey. There was doubt until the very last minute as to whether she would be able to come to the chapel. She made it, and was wheeled in. Many of her friends had come for the service, few if any I suspect were regular churchgoers. Salomey was in good form. She told me that she wished to be baptized and confirmed because she wanted 'to do one thing that is significant in my life.' She then demanded that we sing. 'What shall we sing?' I asked. ' "O Jesus, I have promised to serve thee to the end",' she responded brightly. There was not a dry eye in the house!

On Easter Day I told Salomey's story in prison. As I shook the hands of prisoners leaving to go back to their cells, many paused and said, 'Tell that Salomey I'm praying for her.' Salomey died a few days later. Through her suffering she had done something significant with her life, and borne witness to the possibility of hope. Of course it doesn't explain the apparent meaninglessness of it all, the waste of life, but it speaks in some small way of the God who meets us in the midst of apparent futility, and brings true joy.

As I reflected on Salomey's story, I found many places where it had spoken of God. It reminded me of the significance of each day; that in life nothing is certain, but that each moment is to be valued for itself. Once again I saw that it is possible to look death in the face and not to be afraid of it; that it is in fact the gateway to something of greater significance. As I shared the story in prison, I saw God touch the hearts of people in compassion, and for a moment, in that most invulnerable of places, make them vulnerable. I saw her suffering lead others to prayer, to solidarity, even to faith. A dying woman gave to us all a hope and a challenge to order our lives as if we were *in extremis*, but also provided the opportunity on Easter Day to re-evaluate just how much we do believe in a God who in raising Jesus from the dead also gives life to our mortal bodies.

Of course none of this gives an ultimate answer to the philosophical question about the meaning of suffering. Neither is that my purpose. I, too, am on a journey. For my philosopher colleague there is not sufficient intellectual rigour to provide the clincher to convince him of the need, or possibility, of believing in God. By reflecting spiritually, one cannot ultimately take refuge from hard questions, but often such reflections enable us to find in the day-by-dayness of life some hope and meaning in the midst of grief and loss.

'WHERE IS GOD? . . . CAN WE FIND HIM?'

Recently I visited a local hospital. It was in the aftermath of clamour in the popular press for information concerning body parts of dead children, and although this hospital was, in the words of its chaplain, 'squeaky clean', people were anxious. During the few hours I was there various senior staff spent time with me privately, sharing the difficulties they faced, the huge moral dilemmas presented to them daily, the conflict of ideologies, the struggle with meaning and purpose.

Their experience was epitomized by the account of a friend who was leading a workshop on the Book of Revelation in the hills outside São Paolo in Brazil some years ago. People were arriving from their work, many had been on the road since dawn. The opening mass began with a song in Portuguese, 'We are arriving . . . '. As it concluded, the facilitator asked, 'Where are you coming from?' 'What are you arriving for?' One woman, a nurse, weeping uncontrollably, said that she had come from a hospital. Her haunting memory is of the sacks of foetuses she witnesses day by day stacked outside her office. 'Where is God?' she wailed. Gently, the leader responded, 'I don't know . . . Can we find him?'

So often in our understanding the mystery of suffering we start with the way things are, the extraordinary ordinariness of things. The group of people of which this nurse was a member, were gathering to do some biblical reflection on Revelation. The word 'revelation', in the Bible at least, is one which has to do with God becoming known in historical, verifiable acts. We do our theology out of our experience. When the question is asked, 'Who is God?', the answer is given in reference to history: the God of Abraham, Isaac, Jacob; or in the story of Jesus of Nazareth. In other words we discern God in the stories of others who have discerned God before, and we test our experience against it. If God has historically been found in the concrete, the acts of liberation, the setting free, the opening of the eyes of the blind, the releasing of captives, then can we find God there today?

I was not privy to the outcome of the reflection on the plight of the woman who cried out, 'Where is God?' But by beginning with an honest response to the awful reality faced by the nurse day by day, possibilities were opened up for discerning God's presence through the sharing of experience, as well as listening to the insight of Scripture. On the death of my friends' baby, I was not only privy to their quest, but had to do my own reflection on 'where God was' at this time of inexplicable suffering. Part of the answer came in discovering once again God who is present in the compassion, the longing for the end to suffering, the anger at the loss, and so on. Such insight should not be belittled, for when God is discerned like this, then other possibilities are opened up. One is the very real possibility of seeking to live one's own life more passionately and compassionately; to strive with others to both understand and work for an end to all unnecessary suffering and dying. Another possibility is to understand one's own anger, even anger directed at God, or through transference on to some other god-like person, and to be released from it, learning to refocus rightful anger more appropriately.

The nurse, who daily encountered the gruesome after-effects of the heartless disposal of unwanted foetuses, may well have been able to find God in her own anger and grief by turning them into fresh energy to campaign and work for a more humane policy over abortions. Discerning where God is, and who God is, must by the very nature of things leave us open to the possibility of surprise. For God to be God requires that God cannot be contained or limited by any single definition, or indeed experience.

WHERE HAS HUMANITY GONE?

During a visit to Malawi in 1993 I had my first contact with the reality of AIDS in Africa. I was visiting a hospital. Inside were as many beds as could be fitted into the wards. On the beds lay those who were most sick and closest to death. Underneath lay those who would occupy the beds once the present occupants had died. Outside on the veranda were those who were not yet too sick. It was an apocalyptic scene. The heat, the smell, the cramped and crowded conditions, put me in mind of descriptions of medieval plague houses. I found myself having to face questions not only about the treatment of such people, but about my own attitude. Somewhere deep within myself I discovered a prejudice that believed that 'these people were used to all this, and it wasn't as bad for them as it would be for Westerners like me.' I also found myself facing the huge sense of denial that surrounds AIDS in so many places.

When sometime later I had become all too used to the phenomena of AIDS, I visited a high school for girls in Matabeleland, Zimbabwe. Sitting on the dried earth, shaded from the sun we talked with members of the sixth form. They were all very bright, delightful young women. They talked of their ambitions, their hopes and dreams. None of them mentioned marriage and having a family. One woman wanted to be an accountant, another a doctor, still others a teacher, a pilot. 'And I,' said one girl smilingly, 'want to build the planes she flies.' All recognized the problems of their nation, many spoke frankly about their own role in the future. 'Someone has got to do something about the way things are,' they said, 'and if not the men, then the women.'

As our visit drew to a close I spoke to the head teacher and told her how excited and impressed I had been with this group of young people and their ambitions. Quietly she said, 'Bishop, most of those girls will be dead by the time they are forty.' A while later, a priest spoke to me about his visit to a school where he was to give a talk on sexual fidelity. As he waited to speak to the head, he fell into conversation with a haematologist, who had in her hands a report for the school, in which she was reporting that ninety per cent of the pupils were suffering from infected blood.

In the *undersong* of suffering I began to realize the degree to which it is possible to dissociate oneself from the pain and isolation of others. My own initial reaction at the hospital was in itself a form of denial. Assuming that somehow these victims of AIDS, and the conditions in which they were being treated until they died, was somehow all right for them, exposes in microcosm the degree of apathy and unresolved prejudice with which we regard not only this dreadful illness, but the whole continent of Africa in which it is rife. It was in the encounter with the young women in the sixth form that I realized what this is actually costing the continent in the loss of potential. I found myself asking, 'How is it possible to hope in this environment?'

AIDS is as much a by-product of colonialism and apartheid as it is of cultural attitudes to women within a strongly patriarchal society. Yvonne Vera, who is the Director of the National Art Gallery in Bulawayo, is an international author of repute. Much of her writing is based upon the communities in which she grew up and still lives today. She spoke to me of the bitter-sweet flavour of township life, particularly in the days of racial classification and the effective division of society into those who have and those who have not.

One of her stories traces the history of AIDS, when she recalls how young black men returned from fighting in the Second World War, when they had been sent to Burma, Italy and Germany. Many returned injured, permanently disabled. As Yvonne Vera has put it, 'as soldiers not heroes, blind with mistrust and dizzied by evident defeat, which belonged only to their particular experience.'[2] There were no war pensions, no securities. Racial classification, enforced ghettoization, and the removal of fit men to work in mines and live in hostels hundreds of miles from home, often for years at a time, led to the disintegration of marriage and family as recognizable institutions for many. The incidence of incest became almost commonplace. Such incest is not necessarily parent-natural child abuse, but is often conjugality between informal parent-child relationships, where a child who is the product of another union, but who lives in the same household, is the victim.

The problem continues. Driving around a Harare township a few months ago I observed some new buildings. 'That is where the young couples live until the men die,' the local priest told me. In Nketa township, while celebrating the opening of a new church at which I had laid the foundation stone some two years ago, I 'blessed' some three hundred children, of whom the majority were AIDS orphans, many being looked after by siblings often only a few years older than themselves.

What is being experienced here is a silent genocide. A suffering at which the world is conniving by what Yvonne Vera has called 'that most devastating of divisions – the human into the inhuman'. Of course there are particular actions that national governments and their citizens need to take to stem this pandemic, and there has been much burying of head in the sand by both political and church leaders. But there are international implications and responsibilities to be taken. After a century in which holocaust and genocide became all-too-familiar terms, it becomes imperative that we listen to the voices who have direct experience of such horrors.

The Jewish philosopher, Irving Greenberg, reflecting on the *shoah* that included the horrors of the extermination centres of Europe, said, 'no statement theological or otherwise should be made that cannot be made in the presence of burning children.'[3] We may substitute other adjectives for 'burning' without losing the power of this statement – in respect to the devastating plight of AIDS and other victims around the world. Greenberg believes that nothing less than 'a call to all humans to end the holocaust' will make a future for humanity possible. By this I understand him to mean all holocausts, whether caused by wars, genocide, or AIDS.

The Judeo-Christian tradition has long held to the doctrine of free will. Free will enables us to choose evil as well as good. Simply, what Greenberg demands is that we exercise such in favour of ending the inhumanity of mindless acceptance of the disposability of whole generations of men, women and children. We are quick to ask questions as to the whereabouts of God when evil emerges as the result of inhumanity to humanity, but we are more reticent to ask, and demand of ourselves an answer, 'Where has humanity gone?'

TOWARDS COVENANTAL RESPONSIBILITY

Humanity cannot cope with too much reality. Writing this chapter reminds me of that, for in a sense it raises so many questions, and within the journey of my own spirit has to date provided all too few answers – whether the realities are the sufferings caused through the complex matrix of circumstances that have produced the AIDS pandemic; or that created the environment for the death camps of Europe; or that created the needless suffering of the children I witnessed in Saddam Hussein Children's Hospital in Baghdad, dying of leukaemia and other cancers, not only as a consequence of the disease, but of the bloody-minded bureaucracies of the UN Sanctions procedures and the intransigence of the Iraqi government towards its own people.

If humanity is to have a future, we must find the courage to be a different kind of people. Greenberg's call to 'stop the holocaust' was made from within a tradition. As a Jew he understands that everything holds together in history, and he places the primary responsibility upon his own people by calling 'the people of Israel to rise to a new unprecedented level of covenantal responsibility.' For Greenberg, that responsibility is to work for the abolition of the matrix of values that supports genocide, wherever and however it is experienced.

By implication Greenberg recognizes that this task must find its energy from within faith traditions, even if it is to be implemented by peoples of all faith and those who declare none. His opening appeal for 'all humans' is refocused in his call to 'the people of Israel'. He sees 'Israel', whether literally or metaphorically, as carrying an understanding of both the human and the divine. He sees co-operation and mutual responsibility as the essence of covenant, and integral to the task of ending racism and genocide. Greenberg challenges me because he comes so close to embracing the vision of humanity enunciated by Jesus Christ. However much has been lost in the darkness lit only by the fires of burning children, what has emerged is a common understanding that if humanity is to have a future, its future is repentance: a turning from obsession with racial, religious, or economic superiority, towards a single humanity in which truly each is the other's keeper.

Christians are often described as 'the new Israel' and, like the Jews, our perception of God is determined by covenant. This 'new' covenant for the 'new Israel' is marked by the shedding of blood. But the purpose of the shedding of blood is the ending of all bloodshed. The blood that is shed to make the 'new' covenant is that of Christ, Son of man, Son of God. With his death the rubicon has been crossed. Here in a single individual is gathered up all the hatreds and divisions of humanity, which are killed off once and for all. Inhumanity finally achieves its goal of killing God in a cosmic act, perpetrated at a single moment in history. No other hatred is possible, because all hatred has been taken into the One in whom all things find their source, and ultimately their being. The miracle of the resurrection, therefore, is not so much in the *how* of it, but that it becomes the means by which God intends to be re-interpreted in his world as the One who loves, forgives and includes. To be disciples of the resurrected Christ is to enter into the covenant that makes no distinctions.

For me, this is the reason why the task of responding to the 'call to all humans to stop the holocaust' is such an imperative. It is not simply a task for Christians and Jews. While Muslims are not a covenant people as such, they do come under the promise made by God to Abraham, that God would be with the people of Ishmael.[4] In the aftermath of the Gulf War, I called together a small conference at Southwark Cathedral of Jews, Muslims and Christians. Together we explored within our faith traditions the significance of peacemaking and the ending of war. I believed then, and even more firmly now, that the level of intransigence in human affairs, and the inhumanity that results, indeed calls for a 'rise to a new unprecedented level of covenantal responsibility.' While I am no authority on other faiths, there is an understanding within Buddhism that the seekers after truth cannot seek their own salvation without regard to the other – 'I cannot be saved unless all are saved. I am responsible for the enlightenment of the other.'

While there may be disagreement over many things, what such faith traditions all teach is a profound respect for humanity. By seeking to live out such aspirations, whether based on covenantal faith or not, there is the possibility that humanity can have a future. As God's people, and in the last analysis all humanity by definition is God's, we need not only to rediscover faith in a God who is indiscriminately loving, but there is an obligation to demonstrate it radically. The Abrahamic covenant offered God's protection to Jew and Arab alike, its development laid responsibility upon God's people to protect and defend the weak and the stranger. The new covenant inaugurated by Jesus Christ is marked by self-giving, atoning love. Such love calls out from our deepest selves the humanity given to us at our birth, when we were created in the image and likeness of God. We are called to a more authentic way of living.

'IF THEY CAN – WHY CAN'T WE ALL?'

In order to 'rise to a new unprecedented level of covenantal responsibility', we need as in all things role models, or exemplars. Most of us do not experience suffering *in extremis*, but it is often the experience of those who do that inspires us to live more authentically. One of the most powerful prayers to emerge from the *shoah* was that of the women at Ravensbruck concentration camp. The prayer was discovered near the body of a dead child in a camp where an estimated 90,000 women and children died:

> Lord
> Remember not only the men and women of goodwill,
> but also those of ill will.
> But do not only remember the suffering they inflicted
> on us,
> remember the fruits we bought, thanks to this
> suffering,
> our comradeship, our loyalty, our humility,
> the courage, the generosity,
> the greatness of heart which has grown out of all this,
> and when they come to judgement,
> Let all the fruits that we have borne be their
> forgiveness.[5]

Such a prayer epitomizes covenant responsibility. The anonymous authors of this deeply moving prayer understood that for a covenant of redemption to have new force and meaning, the values of forgiveness, together with a willingness to see their own suffering as some form of atonement, were needed to replace the distorted values of vengeance and recrimination. In the midst of unspeakable distress, covenantal values emerged: comradeship, loyalty, humility and greatness of heart.

During the 'dirty wars' in El Salvador and Guatemala in the late 1980s I paid a visit as part of a small group of people seeking to investigate human rights violations. It was a war in which there was great political confusion, but the respective regimes in both countries had the backing of the United States administration. Training and equipment were offered to repress so-called sub-versives but, as so often in these situations, it was the ordinary people, often the poorest, who suffered from the ensuing terror. My heart was chilled to read on one wall outside the US Embassy the words, in Spanish, 'Here they plan the deaths of our people.'

Accompanying us on the trip were a number of pastors whose churches in the States had been pro-active in the 'Sanctuary Movement'. Christians in the USA receiving news of the danger and plight of citizens of these churches set about the task of providing a means of escape to, and then protection in, their American parishes. Among those who were pro-active in the protection of vulnerable communities was Joyce Hollyday of 'Witness for Peace'. This group recruited some 3000 Christian peace activists, who would go and stay in villages, and by their presence often deter violent actions. Many of them faced arrest and beatings too. In an interview Joyce did with me for the BBC World Service, she commented, 'In one sense this "witness for peace" process changed everything, and changed nothing. What it provided was a fragile hope for a just and lasting peace.' And that in a sense is the risk, and the paradox of seeking to live a more authentic life of faith of covenantal responsibility.

A contemporary example of this more authentic living is wit-nessed in the 'Women in Black' movement. This international group of voluntary peace-keepers, in their middle age, travel to centres of conflict, seeking to do what often foreign governments promise and fail to do, namely monitor and contest abuses of human rights, defuse violence and challenge programmes of ethnic cleansing. Recently such a group has joined other peace activists in Jerusalem and the West Bank where, according to George Monbiot of *The Guardian*, they have been 'joining demonstrations, staying in the homes of threatened Palestinians, turning themselves into human shields between the Israeli army and its targets.'[6] This group has been standing at checkpoints, noting and photographing illegal prevention of movement, and keeping a list of the names of those arrested. As Monbiot commented, 'the soldiers hate this scrutiny, but whenever the monitors arrive at a check point, there's a remarkable reduction of violence there.'

As all such groups have found, this kind of 'covenantal responsibility' is costly. Many have been arrested, along with local people, and beaten up. They have witnessed the torture of Palestinians in the police stations, and the events have been recorded. Monbiot concludes:

> All this is a long winded way of saying something which in the twenty-first century sounds rather embarrassing: these people are my heroes. They confront us with our own cowardice, our failure to match our convictions with action. We talk about it, they do it. Hell's Grannies are walking through fire. If they can, why can't we all?[7]

'STRUGGLE WITH A RECONCILED HEART'

I do not believe that we will be able to speak convincingly as Christian communities about 'a new level of covenantal responsibility' unless we model community in a new way. Being a covenant people demands being with others. Covenantal responsibility is essentially undertaken in solidarity. Our churches can and must become more than just places for our own succour and comfort. If they do not, then examples of covenantal responsibility, whether in Ravensbruck, El Salvador, or the West Bank, will remain only examples.

The *undersong* of suffering calls us to dare to take sides. We may not always agree on which side to take, but that is a lesser matter. As one commentator writes:

> In my situation that would mean, for instance, that the refugees and asylum seekers who come to our country are

understood as part of the parish, they are invited to live with it, they are accompanied by our parishioners. It would mean the unemployed have a place in the church, that the church is an example to society for the sharing of labour and income. The church would keep the individual and social perspectives of life inseparably together.[8]

And it would mean the voice of the 'not needed' being heard.

There are many who in the face of suffering find it hard to believe in God, but whose own lives exemplify love and compassion, like my philosopher friend. Others find in the midst of great personal pain or loss the capacity to rejoice in God, or at least to know God's presence and comfort. Struggling with the issue of suffering is something we shall have to do all our lives.

A few days ago I visited the Taizé community in France, where young people were arriving by the bus load from all over Eastern Europe and elsewhere. We joined them for their opening act of worship. In the centre of the chapel sat Brother Roger, Taizé's founder and prior. His constant message and vision is for all Christian people to 'struggle with a reconciled heart', and to pay attention to community. 'Alone, you cannot do much for others. Together in community, animated by the breath of Christ's loving, a way forward opens up leading from aridity to a common creation. And when a community is a ferment of reconciliation in that communion which is the church, then the impossible becomes possible.'[9]

9

THE UNDERSONG
OF RECONCILIATION

Outside the United Nations Building in New York is a statue of St George and the Dragon. It is unique because it was presented by the then Soviet Union. The statue itself is comprised of the parts of rockets used by both the former Communist state and the United States as delivery systems for their nuclear missiles. Here are Pershing and SS20s broken and reshaped into a symbol of the conquest of evil, and a dramatic symbol of reconciliation, a literal 'beating of swords into plough shares'. During the twentieth century over 100 million people perished in wars and civil conflicts.[1] At its end, humanity seemed no nearer to resolving its historic conflicts than at its beginning.

Inside the United Nations building on two opposite walls stand two huge mosaics. One pictures hope, joy, celebration; the other fear and oppression. And nearby is a brightly-lit mosaic inscribed with the words 'Do unto others as you would have them do unto you'. In such words there is a dream for humanity: a time when all will be reconciled, and people will live in harmony, joy and hope, rather than in fear and oppression. At the heart of the Christian vision is the profound longing that a day will dawn when 'there will be no more death and no more mourning or sadness or pain'[2] – and when the world of the past will be gone.

Tragically, the Christian religion, while having at its heart the core message of reconciliation, has contributed all too much to the conflicts which lie deep-rooted in the human condition. For many this has provided the 'switch off', the point at which

Christian faith is disowned. I understand that, but for me it has had the reverse effect, for try as I might to find alternative philosophies which carry the possibility of hope of a new order, borne out of compassion and self-giving love, I have failed to find one which touches the depths of the teaching and practice of Jesus of Nazareth. Though I have every sympathy with Friedrich Nietzsche when he observes of Christians, 'they are going to have to look a whole lot more saved if I am to believe their Saviour.'

Reconciliation requires of us something more than the desire for it. Like peacemaking, we cannot expect that people will be reconciled simply because we would like it that way. True reconciliation is the hardest task for humanity to achieve. Most of the time the best we attain is a sort of 'armed neutrality', where we hold to ourselves the weapons of hurt, suspicion, fear and distrust, ready to deploy them at the first opportunity. I speak from experience. Several times already in this book I have hinted at the occasions where, as a Christian minister, I have allowed conflict, anger, pride and sheer bloody-mindedness to impact on relationships in such a way that they have destroyed not only relationships, but the opportunity of sharing a quality of living which I firmly believe Jesus Christ both desires and makes possible.

'RECONCILIATION ... MORE OF AN ATTITUDE THAN AN ACQUIRED SKILL'

Over the years I have been privileged to have some small part in the reconciliation process in Northern Ireland. It began with informal encounters among individuals and groups seeking reconciliation between the communities. One of the most significant was Mary Grant, who at the time was helping to found the Cornerstone community on the Belfast 'peace line'. Life was very raw then, and the burnings, shootings and bombings still the stuff of everyday news. Yet Mary retained hope amidst it all, describing the situation as 'being held somewhere between Good Friday and Easter Day in our lives.' Gradually, small groups from across the divide were meeting together, often simply to share their stories. Many of them came from the faith communities, and

part of the story-telling originated in the elements of their
faith, discussing together with mutual surprise at the common-
ality of their favourite hymns or Bible stories. In time people
began to explore the roots of conflict in their neighbourhoods,
and discovered that the issues of unemployment, poverty and
a sense of being forgotten by the powerful was their common
experience, too.

After one of the most publicized IRA killings, that of two
British soldiers in Andersonstown in West Belfast, I interviewed
Cahal Daly, then the Roman Catholic bishop responsible for that
part of Belfast. Bishop Daly was unambiguous in his condemnation of the murders, but he observed that there had been
a series of events that, while having no intrinsic intentional
connection, nevertheless had a bearing on the tragedy of
Andersonstown. 'Many were born in the Troubles, raised on
the streets of violence, unemployed, harassed by the security
forces – is it any wonder that people turn to violence?' Bishop
Daly remarked.

'Apart from prayer,' I asked Daly, 'what can ordinary Christians in Britain do for reconciliation in Northern Ireland?' The
bishop, a man of immense warmth and generosity, smiled – 'Apart
from prayer?' he queried. 'Surely all prayer reveals our own
complicity, our own prejudice, the complexity of the situation.
Such prayer should lead to repentance that leads us to understand, to be better informed, to be enlightened.'

A little later in our conversation Bishop Daly observed, 'Any
prayer for peace, for reconciliation, must have to do with our own
responsibility to work for reconciliation.' This responsibility to
work for reconciliation 'becomes more of an attitude than an
acquired skill,' says Robert Schreiter; 'it becomes a stance
assumed before a broken world, rather than a tool to repair that
world. Or, put in more theological terms, reconciliation is more
spirituality than strategy.'[3]

I have found the words 'attitude', 'stance' and 'spirituality',
used by Schreiter, to have integrity in the *undersong* of reconciliation. St Paul reflects on something of a conflict view of reality
when he writes about reconciliation. For him reconciliation is
only made effective through suffering, 'making peace through . . .

death on the cross'.[4] The familiarity of the phrase 'death on the cross' disguises for us of a softer generation the cultural, political and penal implications of such an execution. Paul understood the human condition to be one marked out by the brokenness of division, oppression, discrimination and violence, and these – together with the 'ruling forces, sovereignties and powers',[5] each in their own way disguising the victims and hiding the causes of suffering – contributed to his conflict view of reality.

Contemporary Christians in my experience face two dangers: those of a more liberal bent tend to take an over-optimistic view of the world and do not allow sufficiently for the imminence of conflict within the human condition. Those of a more fundamentalist persuasion tend to a despairing view of the world, seeing it not as something for which they bear a real responsibility to seek what Schreiter calls 'a fundamental repair to human lives, especially the lives of those who have suffered', but rather as a trial to be lived through in the hope of a pain and trouble-free life beyond death.

Today there is a loss of a sense of responsibility for others. But perhaps more seriously there is a lack of a sense of sacrifice, and of the cost of true peacemaking that makes the task of reconciliation more difficult in our times. Our religion is essentially respectable, ordered, domestic – even 'a leisure activity', as one priest described it to me recently. As a people we epitomize what Charles Péguy, the French poet and philosopher, once observed, 'Their hands are clean ... but they have no hands.' Or, as on one occasion I heard Gerard Hughes say, 'Once Christianity got respectable, devout people went to the graveyard and eventually to the desert.' There is a certain lack of respectability about taking responsibility for and to others.

Taking a stance towards those who suffer, are discriminated against, or are oppressed, requires a certain carelessness for oneself. Penny Lernoux, a passionate campaigner for human rights in Latin America, an award-winning journalist and writer who died of cancer at the early age of forty-nine, once observed,

'I believe that those who seek a new path, whether in the church or secular society, should not expect roses, but must

be prepared to endure the prophet's life in the desert . . .
Sometimes it is hard . . . but I also believe it is the only way
to remain steadfast to Christ's vision.'

The attitude, stance and spirituality of reconciliation is essentially
a prophetic one, and touches every part of our lives.

'CHRIST RECONCILES LIFE'S OPPOSITES . . .'

I observed earlier the African feminist theologian Khumo
Nthlag's reflection of Christ as one who

reconciles life's opposites, rich and poor, black and white,
male and female. In uniting the most basic pair of opposites,
male and female, in his own person living out the consequences of that in a fully integrated personality, Jesus has
not only shown us the way, but has enabled us to integrate
all the opposites that conspire to pull us apart, through his
Spirit in us.[6]

My own journey to the work of reconciliation in uniting that
'most basic pair of opposites, male and female', somewhat paradoxically began when I had to face, at the time of my marriage,
the innate sexism with which my upbringing had endowed me. I
am grateful for the companionship of one of the sanest and saint-
liest women in helping me to face my own machismo. Sexism is
that which takes away the proper complementarity of the sexes.
I think the term 'sexism' has softened the rather harder term
'misogyny'. Misogyny is the hatred of women, and I believe it is
much deeper in our psyche than we dare admit. Anthony Clare,
psychiatrist and broadcaster, has observed that

all men, myself included, do not just love women. We do
not see them only as colleagues, friends, lovers, as sexually
desirable, physically attractive, mentally stimulating. We fear
them, hate them, marginalise them, denigrate and categorise
them. And we continually strive to dominate and control
them. The call to us as men at the beginning of the twenty
first century to turn away from violence, to get in touch

with our feelings, to express our fears and inadequacies, is a doomed call if it is made predominantly by women.[7]

I was brought up with certain expectations of the role of women which, together with a religious outlook that denied women rights in the Church, laid upon them obligations, and all too often made them bear responsibility for sin – particularly of the sexual variety. I confess that much of my early opposition to the ordination of women in our Church was barely disguised misogyny, and I suspect this is the case for many present opponents, and that such misogyny is much deeper within our psyche than we dare to admit. Ann Thurston, a Catholic theologian, observed at a conference in Dublin during 1995 that while she wanted to see the ordination of women into the Church, 'I don't want women sucked into the same clerical culture as men. Without women at a sacramental level, women are diminished,' she said. 'Ministry and community are inextricably connected. The ordination of women and the transformation of structures belong together. We are equal but different.' It is the failure to understand equality in difference that leads to the dividing wall of separation that is required to be breached.

Our obsession with sex, the prevalence of pornography, even on mainstream channels and easily accessible magazines, has contributed to this misogyny. Part of the contemporary tragedy is that the power of libertarianism in sexual matters has led women to be complicit in their own self-abnegation, by being forced so often to define themselves by their sexuality, rather than their complementary humanity.

The issue of reconciling life's 'most basic pair of opposites' profoundly affects our approach to all other areas of reconciliation. The dangerous myth of the seductive woman has led to the perpetual myth that others are to blame for what goes wrong. For a number of years I was vicar of a St Mary Magdalene church. Above the entrance was a beautiful small stained glass window of a woman pouring oil over the feet of a man. The implication of the picture was that this was the 'great sinner' who came looking for Jesus to experience forgiveness and acceptance. It was not a big connection, given the title of the church, to equate the woman with Mary Magdalene, out of whom Jesus 'cast seven demons'. During my incumbency of this parish, I began to read more widely about Mary Magdalene, and discovered how much a patriarchal Church had heaped upon her, particularly between the fourth and seventh centuries. No biblical evidence exists for the Magdalene having been the woman who anointed Jesus' feet. Yet by the seventh century she had been classed as the 'great sinner' by the then pope, and her seven demons had been upgraded to being associated with sexual vice and perversion!

The Magdalene and the haemorrhaging woman spoken of by the Gospel writers both become archetypical of all the myths that have made women responsible for seducing or infecting many, whether psychologically, emotionally or literally through disease and viruses such as AIDS. Jesus' insistence in the Gospel story on obtaining an answer to the question in the midst of the crowd – 'Who touched me?'[8] – enabled not only the truth about the woman's faith to be exposed, but also the truth that the new social order Jesus came to establish was of equal status for all.

It seems to me that the single most important element of any credible practice of faith in the coming century has to embrace the vision of a reconciled humanity, not in some time that is yet to be, but within the very ordinariness of the now. Recently I was in Zimbabwe in a township where many people were hungry because of the current crisis in the economy. As we delivered sacks of mealie-meal to some of the most vulnerable families in the community, I entered squalid shacks, little bigger than a king-size double bed, where in rude simplicity as many as a dozen people shared the living space. Most of the households were held together by women, both they and their children widows and orphans from the AIDS pandemic that has swept across Africa.

Any talk of reconciliation between 'life's opposites, rich and poor, black and white, male and female', remains only so much pious comment until it impacts upon the most vulnerable of those divided on all fronts. Whenever I am confronted by the awesomeness of these realities, it seems to me that most of the things that appear to divide our affluent Western Christianity are self-indulgent and totally without significance. Yet, at the same time, those things which divide us prevent us from addressing the failure of humanity to fulfil the dominical instruction 'to cultivate and take care of [the garden]',[9] that is creation, and all that is in it.

'WHERE IS THE LINE OF PERVERSITY DRAWN ... ?'

It is so often what makes us afraid that keeps us divided, and it does take courage to face within ourselves the places of fear and repulsion. In his *Cure of the Soul*, Thomas Moore observes that seeking to understand what divides us requires an understanding of what is perverse. 'Where,' he asks, 'is the line of perversity drawn for you? Where is the place where you come up against your own fear and repulsion?'

Whenever I search into my soul for answers to my prejudice, I am often shaken by the depth of hostility I find to people who are different from me. I am disturbed, too, at the level of violence that emerges when my integrity as a human being is threatened by something that I simply do not understand or have not learned how to value. Dealing with our own fears and repulsions is essential in the reconciliation process.

Recently we have had a report on institutional racism in the diocese where I am a bishop. It has been an important exercise, and predictably has received a mixed reaction, for both good reasons and bad. Like most reports it is strong on analysis and short on prescription. The concept of 'institutional racism' was first used in the Macpherson Report into the death of the black teenager, Stephen Lawrence, in South London. It is a phrase that may well be accurate, but it defies easy understanding, and frequently leaves people in the institutions so identified feeling powerless and uncertain of what is expected.

One of the problems that we face today is that of 'political correctness', which has become something of a tyranny. It is hard when dealing with any issue today to escape from the tyranny that inevitably goes with the issue at stake, whether it is sexism, racism, homophobia or whatever. But perhaps when issues of such complexity and power as these are being addressed, the stew of emotions they stir up means that there is inevitable excess, and part of that excess is the tyranny of political correctness. But somehow that has to be broken.

Our society has become increasingly a 'blame culture'. Many reports on racism in different organizations have been made in recent years. Most focus on the failure of organizations and institutions to achieve racial equality at all levels. Undoubtedly such observations are true more often than not. However, in human relationships, if we focus on failure, for the most part we continue to fail. We need to find ways of affirming what is positive, good and life-giving – then concentrate on that which needs addressing.

Visiting one of Washington, DC's black ghettoes in the 1980s, where race riots had recently left many dead and a continuing legacy of anger and resentment against the predominantly white authorities, I talked to one white pastor, Tom Nees. We shared together what was involved in finding the basis for racial reconciliation. Initially Tom said that white people's concern for reconciliation was fraught with incipient dangers, and he felt that many prejudices would simply be reinforced on both sides.

A primary task, Tom said, was 'consciousness raising'. By this he meant people needing to make sufficient time to listen to one another, to work towards overcoming the stereotyping of culture and background. He said that when he was with a group of people who were reluctant to tackle the issue either directly or indirectly, if it was a secular group he would ask, 'Can you get together without killing each other?' If the group came from a faith community, he would ask whether there was anything within their faith stories that could help them to begin to deal with their cultural attitudes. Somehow within our faith communities we have to return to the stories that give us insight into dealing with such matters. Prejudice is significantly addressed in the Book of Jonah; the task of reconciliation in Micah; culture in the Samaritan stories of the Gospels, and so on.

In our blame culture, language has become increasingly emotive, even reckless to the point at which at times it is meaningless. The term 'racism' falls into this category. What is often meant is 'white racism'. I speak for myself when I say that, as with my innate misogyny, I have had to deal with the prejudice of my upbringing on matters of race. But there is the world of difference between white people who are allies of racial progress and who seek to do right, and that hard core of racists whose attitude stultifies progress, often among the most fearful in our community. As a Church, and as bishop in the Church, I am committed to critiquing our role in institutional practices that prevent racial equality. But equally, I want to celebrate the vibrant life and commitment of people of all ethnic minorities in our churches in the inner city and suburbia.

What has been rightly required of white people has been a measure of self-critique in respect of their attitudes to minority ethnic groups. 'Whiteness,' said Tom Nees, 'is seen as a curse rather than a blessing for black people. Black people find it really difficult to be around white people because of history and the range of attitudes and feelings that have prevailed over the years.' For me this was an eye-opener. I spoke to him about the way black people greeted me on the street. We observed that white folks mostly passed one another by without noticing each other. 'By and large, because black people are a minority and historically victims, they are more aware of people as people. When you are minority you pay attention – you don't if you are in the majority.' I believe there needs to be an ongoing self-critique, a realization that black people have seen themselves as commodities, or subjects of oppression. Being liked, and being accepted, is an issue for minority groups. 'We want you to be our friends,' said one woman, following some race awareness training for our senior staff. Of course friendship cannot be coerced, and in a sense it cannot be trained for either – though to some degree acceptance can, and everything has to have a starting point.

MOVING BEYOND BLINDNESS

I observed earlier on the question of language, and in particular the term 'racism' as being more often than not a euphemism for 'white racism'. In conversations I have had with individuals and groups within our black communities in particular there is emerging an awareness that racism is colour blind. As one pastor observed, 'I have witnessed just as much resistance among blacks to bridge building with whites as vice versa.' And referring to some words of his co-pastor, he observed, 'Growth for us black folks means no longer being obsessed with the blindness of our white brothers at the expense of tolerating our own.'[10] In addition, many black communities are seeing the dangers of materialism, individualism, and something of a crisis in gender relationships, as doing as much harm within the communities as racism.

It would be easy to concentrate on failure, to be overburdened with what remains to be done. What I find hopeful in the *undersong* of racial reconciliation is that the issues are being faced. All, both black and white, need to continue the quest towards answering the questions: what are we doing right, and what do we still need to do right? There is a growing awareness in all Christian communities that prejudice affects us all and is contrary to the gospel we espouse, which calls us to the struggle for racial justice.

For six years I was Director of the United Society for the Propagation of the Gospel. This society, founded in 1701, was one of the missionary bodies most associated with the colonialism of the eighteenth and nineteenth centuries. Christian mission tends to reflect the culture of the time, rather than define the culture. In the year I am writing, the Society celebrates some 300 years of work. Like all such bodies over the years, it has embraced the prevailing mores and theological outlook current at the time. In 1712, for instance, the SPG (as it was then called) was bequeathed a plantation on the Caribbean island of Barbados with 'three hundred slaves in perpetuity'. Such a possibility seems to us today to be unthinkable, but at the time the Church had accepted a theology of slavery, and the Society saw it as more important that it should support the British government's economic policy in the West Indies than challenge the brutal reality of slavery. Nearly 300 years later, in the 1970s and 1980s, the Society's publications were banned in South Africa, and many of its missionaries under house arrest because of its opposition to apartheid!

I quote this piece of history because it seems to me to be particularly significant in trying to understand what I want to call the *undersong* of reconciliation. Clearly there is a world of difference between the kind of theology that justified the possession of slaves by a Christian mission agency and that which informs the critical, not to say political, stance against the injustice of institutionalized racism found in South African apartheid. The transition from a theology of slavery to a theology of liberation was, of course, an incremental process. Little evidence exists within the history of the Society or the Church of any kind of apology for slavery – though in a lecture I gave at Codrington College, Barbados, the site of the former plantation, I indicated that such action was appropriate.

ACCEPTANCE IS THE ATMOSPHERE OF HUMANITY

True reconciliation cannot begin without a measure of acceptance, and an environment for that has to be created. For a number of years, my friends Canon Roy White and Canon Judy Rees and I facilitated a series of workshops on renewing the Church. Judy's opening address usually included some words from Jürgen Moltmann:

> When others look at us in a friendly way, we feel alive and vital. When others recognise us just the way we are, we feel fulfilled. And when we feel accepted and affirmed, we are happy, for we human beings need acceptance just as birds need air and fish water. Acceptance is the atmosphere of humanity. Where acceptance is lacking, the air becomes thin, our breathing falters, and we languish. Therefore we are repulsed by the indifferent glance, hurt by disregard, and humanly destroyed when others deny us.

Judy would conclude her introduction with these further words, 'It is, of course, relatively easy for us to accept each other when the others are just like us and want what we want. But it is a different matter to accept others when they are different from us and want something other than we do.'[11] Moltmann, a German, wrote his book with relationships between Christians and Jews in mind. He observed that Paul's 'Accept one another as Christ accepted you'[12] speech was made in the light of the Jew/Gentile controversy, where Jewish Christians saw themselves as 'superior' to the Gentile Christians, even though by this stage they were already in the minority.

Accepting one another remains a priority for all who would

engage in reconciliation. Tragically, what Moltmann observed nearly two decades ago about the Church is as true now. 'Even in church what hurts most is our lack of human relationships. The worship services in which we participate every Sunday morning themselves remain devoid of genuine human contact. We scarcely know each other with any mutuality. We do not even consider it very valuable to create community with each other.'[13] Yet it is in the creation of community that the reality of reconciliation becomes possible.

Some years ago I visited Vlakfontein township, near Johannesburg in South Africa. Here for many years a priest, Jeremy Platt, had worked. He had served in the Second World War as a pilot in the South African Air Force. During one flight he had been compelled to land behind enemy lines because his plane ran out of fuel. Facing imminent capture, he realized that he had failed to turn on the reserve tank. He took off for freedom. After the war he worked as a merchant seaman, 'found God', gave up all his possessions and became a member of the Community of the Resurrection, an Anglican religious order that worked for many years in South Africa. Platt was uncompromising in his self-denial, and critical of his religious order's failure to live in poverty, and eventually he left it to live in Vlakfontein.

He would sit beside the roadside, wait and pray, talking with any who passed by. Soon he began to provide basic foods for mothers and children, a small workshop, and much else beside. His inspiration was a mystic, Charles de Foucauld, who had practised a solitary life, seeking to live among the poor. Charles de Foucauld summed up his philosophy by saying, in his own writings, 'the whole of our existence, for the whole of our lives, should cry the Gospel from the roof tops . . . not by our words but by our lives.'

Community tensions between the African National Congress and Inkatha were rising in the township. His stability of presence often ensured that dangerous situations did not get out of hand. When he died, his funeral took place in two stages: firstly in the township, then more elaborately elsewhere. His body had been brought early in the morning to Vlakfontein. Overnight there had been violence. One of the community leaders gave an oration saying, 'I am not a Christian, but he led us as a community. He didn't live and die here for people to fight each other.' Later a memorial slab was laid in the neighbourhood and, for a time at least, the respect in which he was held kept the peace.

What both Platt's and my own experience lead me to observe is just how hard genuine reconciliation is. I suspect within the order he was, for a time at least, a real thorn in the flesh. His idealism and personal commitment to a rigorous option for the poor made him impatient with others who could not follow, yet his work in the township was profoundly one of reconciliation.

SEEKING PEOPLE OUTSIDE MY OWN CULTURE

I find people like Jeremy Platt offer inspiration in the calling to be an agent of reconciliation. However, few people are either called or able for such commitment. Most of us in the day-by-dayness of life have to make simpler, more matter-of-fact choices. For myself, I began many years ago to seek out people from outside of my own narrow cultural group, and I discovered in them something which has been put very well by Barry Lopez,

> a desire to love, and be loved, to experience the fierceness of human emotions, and to make a measure of the sacred part of one's life . . . I've found the most dependable way to pre-serve these possibilities is to be reminded of them in stories. Stories do not give instruction, they do not explain how to love a companion or how to find God. They offer instead, patterns of sound and association, of event and image. Sus-pended as listeners and readers in these patterns we might re-imagine our lives.[14]

It is that re-imagining of our lives, often through story, that is at the heart of the undersong of reconciliation. For many years I avoided watching *Schindler's List*, a film about the work of Oskar Schindler, a businessman who bargained for the lives of Jews condemned to die in Hitler's deaths camps. I eventually watched it one Good Friday. It is a film which exposes what happens when one group of people regard themselves as superior to another. At one point the commandant of a work camp remarks to his

Jewish maid, with whom he is besotted and yet to whom he is brutally cruel, 'I know you are not fully human.' Such a statement blows the mind, and yet the antecedents of dehumanizing and demonizing others are rarely far from our subconscious. When communities are divided on racial, religious or economic grounds, stereotyping borne of ignorance of the 'other' happens all too quickly.

During a visit to the Holy Land I went to the community of Yad Saleem. In 1972 Father Bruno set out to form a community of Jews and Christian and Muslim Palestinians. For the first six years no one came, so that by 1978 Bruno offered God what he said was 'one last chance'. What he sought was a community who would not only look at religion, but at history. Today some forty families live together, though no Palestinians from the West Bank and Gaza can live there, because of current Israeli law. This community exists to provide a model for living together, in itself an act of witness to the reconciling God present in all three religious traditions. A school, which is bilingual, exists for Jews and Palestinians and has become a place where the young learn to live together, and are inspired to work for peace. But above all, Vad Saleem is a place where silence is encouraged – 'For you and God . . . one minute of silence' reads a sign within the prayer room.

One of the members of the community shared his experience with us: 'I met Jews for the first time when I went to university aged nineteen. Here I learned how much stereotyping there is between communities.' Central to the experience of both Jews and Palestinians were the wars of 1948 and 1967, but it was a subject neither could address with the other. 'When Jews celebrate Independence Day, Palestinians and Arabs are reminded of the catastrophe that spelt out for them. It was in the light of all this that we set out to create a centre where people could listen to each other, in order to bring the process of reconciliation.'

The name 'Vad Saleem' literally translated means 'hard peace'. It is an appropriate name for the task of reconciliation. For reconciliation calls for the rehumanizing of those who have been regarded as 'less than human'. It means hearing and understanding what one group's celebration of Independence can mean to those who have been victimized in the process.

WE NEED THOSE WHO REFUSE TO
BE VICTIMS

What the Easter story exposes us to, particularly in the resurrection of Jesus, is a humanity set free from all superiority and inferiority. He is the crucified and risen victim and, as such, invites deep conversion from those who follow him. Ours is increasingly a victim society. As James Alison has put it, 'adoption of the role of the victim [is] one of the key moves in modern society if you want to establish your credentials, and make space so as to be tolerated.'[15] When we adopt the role of victim, we put alongside that experience such words as 'innocent', 'guilty', 'we', 'they'.

Where Good Friday takes us is into the remembrance that we are all children of violence, whether expressed in physical ways, through anger or self-justification. When we allow ourselves to be victims and award ourselves 'sacred status' because of our church tradition, social position, ethnicity or gender, it becomes a very potent form of emotional blackmail. The Easter event offers us 'knowledge of Jesus, the crucified and risen victim [and he] makes a difference here. For if you know that you know the crucified and risen victim, you know that you are not the victim.' Grasping this is the key to reconciliation, for when we are truly converted to Jesus, we 'no longer need to define ourselves against anyone at all.'[16]

In our victim society, we need those who refuse to be victims, and the Church can be made up of such people because we 'know the crucified and risen victim'. When we submit ourselves to be converted to Jesus, whether as victim or perpetrator of violence, we become truly exemplary and offer hope, rather than fear, to those like us who are made in the likeness of God.

In 1989 I was on a silent seven-day retreat at Penmaenmawr in North Wales. I had been advised not to read the papers nor listen to the radio during this time. I had bargained with the retreat conductor that she would let me know if Margaret Thatcher resigned. What I had not bargained for was that it would be the very time when the Berlin Wall came down! One evening my fellow guest, Charles Elliott, and I broke the curfew and walked out onto the beach in the midst of the most magnificent storm. 'Did you hear about the Berlin Wall?' Charles enquired. 'Yes,' I replied, 'I saw it on a newspaper hoarding as I was making my afternoon walk.' 'I told the retreat conductor you would know,' he said, 'because she was wondering whether to tell you!'

In many ways the fall of the Berlin Wall was a pivotal moment, raising the possibility of new thinking, and a new humanity. To understand *reconciliation* from the perspective of the New Testament, the imagery of the wall is helpful. In the letter to the Ephesians, the author is struggling to bring the Christian community into an understanding of the need for reconciliation between Jews and Gentiles and God. He alludes to this peace being achieved through breaking 'down the barrier which used to keep them apart, by destroying in his own person the hostility . . .'[17] The image here is not simply one of a 'hole in the wall', but rather of every stone being removed, taking the building back down to the foundations.

What is required of all of us in the *undersong* of reconciliation is that we face within *ourselves* that enmity which destroys harmony, and prevents the creation of a 'single new humanity.'[18] We need to return to the foundations, particularly those of which Jesus Christ was both a teacher and exemplar. Acknowledging the schizophrenia that exists within our divided humanity, we need to grasp again the possibility of a 'new humanity', not at some time in the future, in the 'wild blue yonder', but now in the ghettoes and sidewalks, streets and neighbourhoods that comprise our daily living.

We cannot underestimate the difficulty of the task of true reconciliation. But there is little doubt that it can be the only focus of mission in the coming century. As the World Council of Churches Seventh Assembly concluded,

> A reconciled humanity and renewed creation is the goal of the mission of the Church. The vision of God uniting all things in Christ is the driving force of its life and sharing. The diversity of cultures is of immediate relevance to the

church's ministry of reconciliation and sharing, for it affects both the relationships within the churches and also the relationships with peoples of other faiths.

10

THE UNDERSONG
OF LOVING

SOME THINGS ARE JUST MYSTERY. Love, and water flowing round a rock are just two of life's mysteries. Both inspire awe and wonder. Out to the West of Donegal in Ireland is Muckros Point. Here the waves that have travelled across 3000 miles of Atlantic meet the shore. We often walk here, and at low tide a flat expanse of rock is exposed. As the waves break, they do so into countless little ravines and gullies. One writer has observed, 'The streaming of water around rock is one of the most complex motions of which human beings are aware. The change from a laminar, more or less uniform flow to turbulent flow around a single rock is so abstruse a transition mathematically that even the most sophisticated Cray computer cannot make it through to a satisfactory description.'[1]

Ours is an age that wants to quantify and measure everything. Everything it seems needs an explanation or a reason. The simple observation of water around rock defies easy answers, and its very simplicity and complexity have been casually observed by us since many of us were children playing on the beach. Love too defies over-definition. It is like water swirling around a rock – abstruse both in its complexity and simplicity. Most of us recognize acts of love when we see them, and yet the motives and the promptings that create them are only in part understood.

The vision of the world God created in the Bible is of an Eden: a world of beauty and splendour in which the whole of creation lives in harmony with itself, and humanity conserves it in a spirit of love towards the Creator. It is a vision of what is known in Hebrew as *shalom*, a concept implying wholeness, harmony and peace. In the opening chapters of Genesis, the picture given is of a world created for interdependence, unmarred by destructiveness and the ravages of human folly. Later in the human story, when the principles of conservation and love for the Creator have been broken, a new vision for humanity is enacted in the person of Jesus. It is one marked by forgiveness and the restoration of the harmonic relationship between created and Creator. All are called to embrace the vision, and those who do are to be inspired by self-giving love exemplified in the person of Jesus Christ.

Since my teens I have been excited and energized by this vision of love. Embracing it has been a lifelong venture, and witnessing how others have entered into it has been both a mystery and a constant source of wonder. Wherever I have travelled I have found the *undersong* of love and loving present in all groups of people. There is a fierce desire to love and be loved. To love and be loved is something sacred, even when it is barely understood. The journey from fear to love is the cosmic journey from one side of the hearth to the other. At the Corrymeela community of reconciliation in County Antrim there is a chapel. It is known as the 'croil', which means both heart and hearth. A place of loving, and place of warming. The *undersong* of loving seeks to take us both to the hearth, and heart of things. To make the cosmic journey from one side of the fireplace to the other, to leave fear behind and embrace that for which we long most – love.

'TILL DEATH US DO PART'

When I met my wife of some thirty-four years we were students. She lived in the north of Ireland and I in the west of England. We courted, as they used to say, mostly by correspondence and phone calls. In the three years of our courtship we were together for barely forty days in total. We were both people of faith. Marriage as a life-long commitment was important to us. We took the plunge, and as relative strangers began our married life together. The months before had been marked by the ups and downs of certainty and doubt: a struggling, on my part at least, to understand at some level what it meant both to be loved and to love in the kind of way that made 'till death us do part' possible.

Tucked away into our respective Bibles lies a prayer that someone gave us for each other when we became engaged. We still have the original bits of paper, thirty-five years on; both privately and out loud from time to time we still pray it:

> That I may come near to her, draw me nearer to Thee than to her; that I may know her, make me to know Thee more than her; that I may love her with the perfect love of a perfectly whole heart cause me to love Thee more than her. And most of all, that nothing may be between me and her, be Thou between us every moment. That we may constantly be together, draw us into a separate loneliness with Thyself . . .[2]

That prayer has, perhaps more than any other, helped me to understand what it means both to love God and to love another. Like most married couples, loving each other through thick and thin has not always been easy. We have had an extraordinary friendship at the heart of our marriage, and perhaps that more than the vagaries of passion or the burden of responsibility has enabled us to find in each other a deep sense of joy and contentment.

Like other couples, too, we have been aware that we could have had interesting, fulfilling relationships with other people during our marriage, but the choice once made, which to many seems like sacrifice, is what marriage is about. Of course, as the Hebrew language understands it, love is knowledge, and knowledge realizes community. To 'know' someone is to love them, for when all the pretence and masking has been removed, we see the person for what they are, and if we are allowed such intimacy then the only response is love. To find love in the 'other' is also to find community, a place of belonging, of warmth, of discernment. Within such there is a certain recklessness, a lack of calculation, a risk taking.

In describing ours as an extraordinary friendship, I do not mean that it is unique. Those who have been through several

decades of togetherness need something more than memories of
what once was to sustain them. As I mentioned earlier, hidden
away in my filing cabinet is the half of a correspondence I had
with my best friend from school days during three months he
spent in Germany. Both of us were very intense about our faith,
and much of the substance of the letters recounts our insights, our
calling each other to pray, and quite a lot about girls! I took a few
minutes out to reread some of them, as I have the voluminous
correspondence between Dee and myself. What is common to
both is hope, the sharing of ideas, aspirations, as well as fears and
doubts. In addition there is the admission that from time to time
the effort of writing has led to times of silence.

In seeking to define friendship, Elie Wiesel says, a friend is

> a travelling companion with whom we re-build the route and
> strive to conquer the impossible, even if only to sacrifice it
> later. Friendship stamps a life as deeply as – more deeply
> than – love. Love can degenerate into obsession, but friend-
> ship never means anything but sharing. It is with friends we
> share the awakening of desire, the birth of vision or a fear. It
> is to friends that we communicate our anguish at the setting
> of the sun or the lack of order, or injustice . . . What is a
> friend? The person who first makes you aware of your own
> solitude and his, and helps you escape it so that you, in turn,
> may help him. It is thanks to him that you can fall silent
> without shame, and unburden yourself without loss of face.[3]

'PUTTING GOD AND LOVE TOGETHER'

In the *undersong* of loving, we all need friendships that are
marked by desire, vision, and the sharing of fears, as well as the
gift to communicate such things. I have been privileged in
the friendships I have had from both men and women that have
formed and transformed me. While I agree with Wiesel that 'love
can degenerate into obsession', I believe there is something
intrinsically different about love, something that rises above both
friendship and companionship. Love takes us into places and
experiences that transcend even friendship, such as suffering,

grief and loss. One poem that expresses this kind of loving for me
is this one:

> I am putting God and love together
> with tiny blue flowers in the wild vetch,
> with my father who can't move any more
> and has given up the idea of time
> in a chair in front of the TV,
> with my mother in that nursing home with her seven
>   strokes;
> and I want to stop now and think about their suffering
> as if they belonged together like a Christmas cactus
> and its pink blossoms. I want to send them rivulets
> and all the sweetness they can hold in their arms.
> I want their grief to matter.
> And I want God to remember them and make up for
>   all of this
> in a sweeping gesture of mercy like warm rain.[4]

I suppose this speaks so powerfully to me because my own
parents died separately and alone. My father couldn't move any
more because of a massive heart attack which killed him 'in a
chair in front of the TV', where he was not discovered for several
days. At the same time my mother, suffering from Parkinson's
and senile dementia, lay unaware in a hospital a few yards from
her home. Like so many children of my generation, I had found
my parents remote and hard to know. But in the years immediately preceding their deaths I had, as I indicated in 'The
Undersong of the Child Within', come to value, appreciate, yes,
and love them. Of course, as a child I had feared their dying, but I
was never sure whether such fear was borne out of love, or the
anxiety of being left alone. Love, it seems to me, has to have
about it that which enables the possibility of 'all the sweetness
they can hold in their arms.' By that I mean something that is
willingly offered, and selflessly given.

Much of my experience has been a 'putting of God and love
together'. Often it has been the simplest of gestures, and love to
be love does not have to be determined by prior knowledge of
the other. Some years ago Dee and a friend were holidaying

by the sea in Hastings with two young children. Tripping, the friend broke her ankle. Nearby sat a couple in a large Jaguar car, the friend's apartment was less than a quarter of a mile away. 'Could you possibly give me a lift?' she enquired. 'There's no room – we cannot help you,' came the reply.

By contrast, my wife, now responsible for both of the children, needed milk for their breakfast. Leaving them for a few moments in a children's playground she went to the local shop, promising to return in fifteen minutes. The shop was managed by a Sikh, and there were long queues. 'When do you close?' Dee asked. 'In ten minutes,' he replied. Dee explained what she needed and her predicament. 'I will stay open until you return with your children,' he told her. When they returned, the shop had sold out of milk. 'We have our own milk,' said the manager, 'and I would like you to have it.' It was just enough for breakfast.

'It takes so much to be a full human being that there are very few who have the enlightenment or the courage to pay the price,' says Morris L. West in *Shoes of the Fisherman*.[5] When we witness humanity demonstrated in loving, then we realize what a beautiful gift we have been given by God, and it is the countless acts of kindness, selflessness – loving – that make it possible for humanity to exist amidst the forces of destruction and futility that ominously decorate our lives.

'I SIMPLY LOVE'

For many years now I have been visiting New York. On my first visit I met Frankie, who manages a deli down on New York's West Side. It is a homely place. Frankie does not spend much on fancy displays, but there is always good coffee, and however long the break between visits, a warm welcome and a fresh pot are put on when I enter the store.

One night in the mid eighties, during my first visit, I was feeling homesick. I stopped off at Frankie's for one of his 'specials'. It took a while to make; all the time he talked to me he watched, and greeted his customers. Most were poor, many on food tokens. One young man began filling his pockets. Frankie noticed, nodded to his son, and a few minutes later the lad was at the raised till counter. By now he had been relieved of his ill-gotten goods, but with courtesy and tact. 'Now my friend,' said Frankie, 'what else do you need? Tell me.' The lad listed a few items, Frankie collected them in a brown bag and presented them. 'You can have anything you need,' he said, 'just ask.'

When I asked him why he did what he did, he replied in his Spanish American, 'I simply love. I love the people.' Frankie too had a severely handicapped wife, for whom he cared with a passionate devotion. What astounds me about people like Frankie is their fidelity, the holding of a simple yet profound vision of love for all humanity, often experienced in its most broken of states. In my occasional encounters with such people, they are always the same, doing the same tasks day in day out, bearing in themselves a loving humility that is the glue that holds fragile communities together. These are the ones who 'have the courage and the enlightenment to pay the price' of being a full human being.

Whether Frankie was a practising Catholic in that he went to church or not, I don't know. What I do know was that the practice of his faith was a constant demonstration of love for the stranger, and those who cringe from power in an increasingly exclusive society. As a Christian who also happens to be a church leader, the Frankies of this world disturb me. I have all too often witnessed within church life a kind of moral self-righteousness, which is passed off as loving, when in fact it is the very antithesis. I was once asked to preach at a church in a new housing development in Singapore. It was in an affluent neighbourhood. I had been attending a conference on mission, and was accompanied by two colleagues. Singapore has found a way of hiding its vulnerable and unacceptable face. I knew that there were many who suffered exploitation in the sub-culture of the society.

WHERE ARE THE 'LITTLE ONES'?

Uncertain of what I should preach about, I asked the folk who accompanied me to look for the 'little ones' and tell me before the service whom they had spotted. Try as we might, we could not identify them. After the service I spoke to a young woman carrying a baby. 'Who are you?' I asked. 'I am nobody,' she replied, 'I am just the maid.' 'That's it,' I thought to myself, 'these are the little ones, the Filipino and Sri Lankan maids and ancillary workers.'

Later that day I was taken out for lunch by a wealthy Christian family. In the car the conversation between folk revolved around working on Sundays. One woman confessed that after lunch she would have to 'work'. Another chastised her saying, 'I'll tell the pastor about you. You should not work on the Lord's Day.' The conversation moved on to discussion as to whose maid had become a Christian. 'How many days a week do your maids work?' I asked. 'Seven,' came the reply, 'but they come with us to church on Sundays.' My courage failed me, and I did not ask them to apply the same criteria to their maids as they did to themselves. What disturbed me was how the 'Christianizing' of their servants was more important to these church people than their practice of love towards them.

For those of us who claim a Christian heritage and to be people faithful to the vision of God for humanity, there is an enormous responsibility to ensure that our lives match our words. For we cannot claim the corner on the heritage of loving without great humility and care. Visiting one of the parishes in my area recently, I was invited to stay to lunch. The church works among the many asylum seekers and refugees who live within its boundaries. Sitting down at table, I introduced myself. People smiled and nodded, and I realized that few if any had any English. Gradually people understood and each said their name and explained where they were from. 'And you?' I said to one young woman. 'I'm Tracey and I'm from Mitcham,' she replied in clear English. We both laughed, because her home was in the neighbouring London borough, and she was the only other English person at the table.

It transpired that with the exception of Tracey all the others were refugees from Eastern Europe. Tracey told me her story. She was a trainee hairdresser, and one day the girl sitting next to her, an asylum seeker, had come to work in her salon. Within a short time they became friends, and Tracey described their relationship as like 'finding my closest sister'. Tracey had listened to her story of persecution, of the difficulties with the immigration authorities, as well as those of her family. She told me that at school she was 'good at English' and she decided to use this gift to help communicate to the authorities and the various social services the plight and needs of her new-found 'sister'.

Tracey's own life was far from simple. She lived on her own in a one-bedroom apartment. During the course of a recent burglary her neighbour had been murdered. Despite pleas for extra security and zero tolerance policing, nothing has happened. Her visit to church that Sunday was her first, yet she spoke of wanting to do more for her suffering friends. I was very moved, and said to her that in her simple obedience to meeting the human need of her 'closest sister' she was doing God's will.

There is a poignant end to this story. Tracey is not her real name. At this moment she cannot be found. Her 'closest sister' was deported with members of her family. Tracey was heart-broken. Her connections with others, including the church, were so tenuous. Her actions were instinctive and motivated by compassion and love. In the end, the powers that caused her to live in fear, and in turn separated her from her new friends, defeated her. Rumour has it that she is on drugs and has given up. No one has yet had time to seek her out.

'LOVE WITHOUT COURAGE AND WISDOM IS SENTIMENTALITY'

When we as Christians speak about love at the centre of our faith, we need to do so with great care, mindful that we are always being judged on our caring for the 'least'[6] in our world. This is serious stuff, because all too often our perception of ourselves as loving communities is misperception. To love the least, the excluded, the 'not needed' in our world requires commitment. To stand with such people frequently means suffering the approbation and criticism of others, even those closest to us. Ammon Hennacy, a Christian anarchist, once observed,

> Love without courage and wisdom is sentimentality, as with the ordinary church member. Courage without love and

wisdom is foolishness, as with the ordinary soldier. Wisdom without love and courage is cowardice, as with the ordinary intellectual. The one who has love, courage and wisdom is one in a million, who moves the world, as with Jesus, Buddha and Gandhi.[7]

We may feel Ammon Hennacy is hard on the 'ordinary church member', but so much of what passes for loving is little more than sentimentality. Earlier, in reflecting on the *undersong* of suffering, I observed that our world demands a new level of covenantal responsibility marked by love, courage and wisdom from the communities of faith. Part of the reason why our communities of faith are not as distinctive as they are called to be lies in their inability to believe that God loves indiscriminately, and as the stories of Tracey, Frankie, and the Sikh shopkeeper quoted earlier demonstrate, God will find ways of revealing that love among the most insignificant, and even marginalized people.

'God is not to be known,' says James Alison, 'unless we grasp the depth of our freedom and unfreedom, unless we give up our fictions about purity or our innocence and become committed to searching out those we exclude and suppress, creating with them the promised community of mutual gift.'[8] There is hard truth here. Whatever grace we may receive from God at either the moment, or within the continuing process of conversion, we remain people who are deeply flawed, neither pure nor innocent, just forgiven. This is both our 'freedom' and our 'unfreedom'. It means, too, that we stand alongside the worst and best of people. Whenever we appear moralistic, 'holier than thou', or indeed see loving God as a higher form of loving than loving our neighbour, we exclude and suppress.

For some years in my youth I had toyed with the idea that God might be calling me to be a missionary. When I met Dee and fell in love with her, we both sensed something of a vocation to serve God, possibly overseas. At one point we were interviewed by a mission society that advised us that if we were to serve with them we would need to give up the idea of marrying for at least seven years! The reason given was that to love God was the highest calling, and the distraction of a lower form of loving, particularly one expressed at least in part in sexual terms, had to be sublimated. Well, young and naïve as we were, we thought, 'If this is what God wants we'll do it.'

GOD HAS CREATED US TO BE WITH ONE ANOTHER

The decision to put off our marriage was as brave as it was foolhardy – and lasted all of a month! A good and wise pastor, on being told of our intentions, threw back his head and roared with laughter – an unexpected, but entirely appropriate response as it turned out. He asked me, 'Do you love her?' On receiving an affirmative, he followed it up by saying, 'Can you imagine sitting seven years from now in some foreign language class a million miles away still not married to her?' I couldn't. He then went on to enunciate a truth which I gratefully grasped then, and have discovered to be eternally true since. The truth is that God has created us to be with one another. Other people are placed in my way in order to be with them, and together with them to find the way to God. By excluding them, I would be excluding God, who is both revealed and fulfilled in them. Needless to say the subsequent decision to marry soon was taken with joy by us both!

In writing this book, while frequently delving into other people's stories, I have endeavoured to speak only out of my own experience of the *undersong*, the life of the Spirit, the 'pull and push of the journey.' There is a danger therefore in the account of someone who believes that the interrelatedness of divine and human love is primarily expressed in heterosexual marriage, should themselves become guilty of the very exclusion that he condemns others for. I have discovered in my journey that relationships between two women, or two men, or between men and women who are not married to one another, or people for whom sexual relationships are not possible because of disability, have nevertheless been relationships in which God's grace has been apparent.

When as a teacher I sought in religious education to teach the difference between the forms of love – *eros*, in which lies the attraction of the other, or *agape*, in which lies the option of a love that does not count the cost – I fell into a basic error. Instead of seeing these two dimensions of love, along with that of *phileo*, the companionship of the other, as being interrelated, I sought to raise one, *agape*, above the others. I only resolved this one day while sitting by a swimming pool in Minorca, when I read the following:

> Our love is embodied in our feelings, our touch, our passion, and our care. If spirituality loses touch with its roots in sexuality, it loses power to form and inform our deepest selves. When sexuality is separated from spiritual develop-ment, it becomes something we use to manipulate, control and harm what we profess to love. When spirituality is separated from our sexuality, it loses the power of personal connection and becomes lifeless – it cannot move us to passionate care for this world.[9]

When we love with the whole of who we are in an integrated, interrelated way, acknowledging our frailty, giving up 'our fictions about innocence and purity', and recognizing that there is a mystery at work despite our dysfunctional human relationships, then we truly discover who God is for us. We discover too that to love God is to love the other, and in the loving of the other is the loving of God, because love is gift. We love because God first loved us, as St John reminds us.[10]

Sometimes the act of loving means leaving things unresolved, some questions unanswered. We simply cannot, nor are we required to tie up all the ends. I love the anecdote that Elie Wiesel tells of Martin Buber, who asked, 'What is the difference between Jews and Christians? We all await the Messiah. You Christians believe he has already come and gone, while we do not. I therefore propose we await him together. And when he appears we can ask him, "were you here before?"' Then Buber paused, and added, 'And I hope that at that moment I will be close enough to whisper in his ear, "For the love of heaven, don't answer."'[11]

'MAY I KNOW THEE MORE CLEARLY, LOVE THEE MORE DEARLY, FOLLOW THEE MORE NEARLY'

Over the years I have been grateful for the correctives offered by friends, particularly those whom one has known literally for a lifetime, and whose insights in younger years have grown into profundity and wisdom in the middle years of our lives. Just before the turn of the century I had been warned about over-busyness, 'burning the candle at both ends'. I had not paid heed, and was paying the price with a bout of nervous exhaustion. A woman friend who has known me from when we were teenagers together and knows of this tendency sent me some words of Leon Bloy: 'In all ages, ardent and magnificent souls have thought that in order to do enough it was absolutely necessary to do too much.' Hardly subtle, it spoke deeply to me, and I recalled with gratitude both the intimacy and the distance that made such an intervention possible.

Like the water round the rock, there is wonder and mystery in all our relationships borne in the *undersong* of loving. In the Coptic Church in Jerusalem there is an apparently insignficant poor old man who prays day and night for the pilgrims who come to the city. Who knows what miracles of loving have been wrought by his prayers? For me, he is an ikon of Christ, who as the writer to the Hebrews has it 'lives for ever to intercede for them.'[12]

This book has been one of encounters, often privileged, often among the anonymous little ones who people our world and frequently offer it hope. Much of my life has been privileged, if not economically, then certainly in the journeys made, the people met, the experiences shared. Along with the privilege has gone responsibility to bear good news to others. Often there have been temptations, chiefly to arrogance and a tendency to think of oneself more highly than one ought. Often illness has been the means by which these temptations have been challenged, and new opportunities given.

For me, the important lesson in the *undersong* of the Spirit has been finding a means for the voice of God to reach beyond all other clamouring voices and experiences and speak to me. Rilke once observed,

> Don't ask anyone to speak about you, not even contemptuously. And when time passes and your name is circulating among men, don't take this more seriously than anything else you may find in their mouths, think rather that it can become cheapened, and throw it away. Take another name, any other, so that God can call you in the night . . . And hide it from everyone.[13]

And I can think of no more fit way of concluding than with my favourite prayer:

> Thanks be to thee, my Lord Jesus Christ,
> for all the benefits which thou hast given me,
> for all the pains and insults which thou hast borne for me.
> O most merciful Redeemer, Friend and Brother,
> May I know thee more clearly,
> Love thee more dearly,
> And follow thee more nearly,
> day by day.[14]

UNDERSONG – CADENZA

'WHAT TUNE IS PLAYING IN THE *undersong* for you?' she asked. 'It will be jazz,' I replied. 'Which piece?' she enquired. 'A small piece of Swedish jazz music called '*Visa fran Jarna*'.[1] 'Why that tune?' 'Because it is simple. It sums up, in a few notes, loss, longing, faith, hope and love. And it was given to me at a time when I needed something to help me to interpret all of them.'

The record cover – and that dates it – pictures a woven bag upon which is embroidered the picture of a steam train. The bag would have been used by Swedish emigrants as they left hunger and poverty for a life in the New World, full of expectation, longings, fears and hope.

It remains one of the ambitions of my life to learn to play jazz piano. Jazz has become something of a parable of living in the *undersong* of the Spirit. As the great jazz trumpeter, Wynton Marsalis, once observed, 'In jazz you project your personality and discover positive and negative things about your personality. Jazz is about projecting your personality, and prizes individuality, but it also places upon you the responsibility to figure out how to put your individuality in the context of a group.'

At its very best that is what the Church is about. It is finding the capacity to express individuality, to discover positive and negative things about yourself, and yet somehow to remain accepted as you grow into the community, taking your share of responsibility in figuring out what you should do and be together. This book has been about the 'pull' and 'push' of the spiritual journey, in the company of others, as it has impacted so far upon me. Within the *undersong* there has been a passion that somehow the Christ, who has accompanied me through it all, can be seen, longed for and known as the source of joy and companionship, the inspiration and the fire to shape this world more humanly than it is.

I have told many stories, but one remains. In the deep mountainous country of China where travellers rarely venture lives a small group of villagers. Approaching the village the visitor's eye perceives only unclimbable cliffs. In reality the cliffs are tiny strip fields clinging to the mountainside where the community's crops are grown. A friend who works for Medicin san Frontières, a medical aid agency, arrived there and called at the local woodworker's house. There, in the simplicity, were the roughly carved figures of a man, a woman and a child. Picking each up, she passed her hand over them, murmuring 'Joseph', 'Mary', 'Jesus'. 'Do you know these people?' asked the astonished woodworker. 'Since 1949 we have had no one to teach us, and we thought we were the only people in the world who knew about Joseph, Mary and Jesus.' 'You are not alone,' our friend replied. And neither are we.

NOTES

PRELUDE – UNDERSONG
1. Phil Cousineau, *The Art of Pilgrimage* (Element, 1998), p. 21.
2. Thomas Moore, *Cure of the Soul* (Piatkus, 1992).
3. *ibid.*
4. Marcel Möring, *The Great Longing* (Flamingo, 1995).
5. William Least Heat-Moon, *Blue Highways* (Pimlico, 2001).
6. Isaiah 30:15, 18.
7. Guillermo Cook, *The Expectation of the Poor* (Orbis, 1985), p. 172. The quote from Orlando Costas is also recorded by Cook.
8. Matthew 6:25.
9. Michael H. Crosby, *House of Disciples – Church, Economics and Justice in Matthew* (Orbis, 1989).

1: THE UNDERSONG OF THE CHILD WITHIN
1. Paul Tournier, *What's in a Name?* (SCM Press).
2. A story told in *Chicken Soup for the Soul* by Jack Cranfield and Mark Victor Hansen (Vermilion, 2000).
3. Marva J. Dawn, *The Hilarity of Community – Romans 12 and How to Be the Church* (Eerdmans).
4. Robert Bly, *Iron John* (Element, 1991).
5. *ibid.*, p. 24.
6. *ibid.*, p. 24.
7. From the Night Office of the Communities of the Sisters of the Church.
8. Exodus 2.
9. Exodus 3:1-7.
10. Genesis 22.
11. Genesis 32:23-33.
12. 2 Timothy 1:7 New King James Version.
13. Ephesians 4:13 (my inclusive translation, based on The Jerusalem Bible).
14. Matthew 5:48.

15. Elisabeth O'Connor is the author of this quote, though apart from my Commonplace Book I cannot find its origin. We met a couple of times during my visits to the Church of the Saviour in Washington, DC in 1987, and her books and writings have influenced me greatly, particularly *Cry Pain, Cry Hope* (Word, 1987).
16. Barry Lopez, *Crossing Open Ground* (Picador).
17. Marcel Möring, *The Great Longing* (Flamingo, 1995).
18. John M. Feehan, *The Secret Places of Donegal* (Mercier).
19. *The Guardian Weekly*, 15 November 1992. Dervla Murphy quoted the article in her book *The Ukimwi Road* (Flamingo, 1994).
20. Psalm 37:25 Revised Standard Version.
21. Lamentations 4:4.
22. Psalm 132:15 Revised Standard Version.
23. Some remarks from a magazine called *Crosscurrents* published in 1984.
24. From an article in *The Guardian*, 22 May 1999, based on the film *Last Days* by James Mole. The account is by Alice Lok Cahana.
25. Revelation 21:3.
26. Daniel F. Romero, 'The Church's Struggle with Diversity', *International Review of Mission*, No. 337 (April 1996), p. 189.
27. Quoted by Walter Wink during a series of addresses to the Churches' Commission on Mission in Bangor in 1994.

2: THE UNDERSONG OF CONVERSION

1. *Sojourners* (March/April 2000).
2. Thomas Merton, *Seeds of Contemplation* (Anthony Clarke, 1972).
3. Genesis 1:27, 31.
4. *International Review of Mission*, Vol. LXXX no. 337, p. 192.
5. Jürgen Moltmann, *Creating a Just Future* (SCM Press).
6. Matthew 19:21; Matthew 19:27.
7. Pablo Richard, *Apocalypse – A People's Commentary on the Book of Revelation* (Orbis, 1996).
8. Joan Chittister, *A Passion for Life – Fragments of the Face of God* (Orbis, 1996).
9. The exhibition was held in the Town Museum, Chepstow, Monmouth.
10. Quoted by Robert Ellsberg in *All Saints* (Crossroad, 1999). This is a compendium of everyday saints for every day of the year.
11. See Matthew 25:31-46.
12. Regrettably I cannot find the source of this quote, though I have a hunch I found it in one of the Maryknoll Mission magazines when I was visiting a Catholic Centre in Toronto in 1992.
13. Luke 6:27-9 (my translation).
14. Bill Cook, in conversation at Salem Mass, 1989.

15. A comment made in a private paper for the Maryknoll Advisory Committee to Orbis, December 1992.

16. *ibid.*

17. Isaiah 30:15.

18. Rian Malan, *My Traitor's Heart* (Vintage, 1991), p. 309.

19. Luke 9:23.

20. Malan, *My Traitor's Heart*, p. 409.

21. John 9:1-3.

22. James Alison, *The Joy of Being Wrong* (Crossroad Herder, 1998).

23. From a private paper for the Orbis Publishing Management Group.

3: THE UNDERSONG OF COMMUNITY

1. Dorothy Day, *The Long Loneliness* from Dorothy Day, *Selected Writings* (Orbis, 1992).

2. Levinas is quoted by Marcel Möring in *The Great Longing* (Flamingo, 1995).

3. David Augsburger, *Caring Enough to Forgive* (Regal Books, 1981).

4. Elisabeth O'Connor, in a private conversation. Elisabeth was a member of The Church of the Savior in Washington, DC, a woman who suffered from the most debilitating arthritis, but was the most creative author and writer.

5. Henri Nouwen, *Clowning in Rome* (Darton, Longman and Todd, 2001).

6. *ibid.*, p. 13.

7. Robert Bly, *Iron John* (Element, 1991), p. 29.

8. Philip C. McGraw, *Life Strategies – Stop Making Excuses* (Vermilion, 1999).

9. John Caputo, *Radical Hermeneutics: Repetition, Deconstruction and the Hermeneutic Project* (Indiana Press, 1988).

10. Eduardo Hoornaert, *The Memory of the Christian People* (Burns and Oates, 1989).

11. Eduardo Hoornaert has offered a helpful concordance on other 'little virtues' – being ready to pass unnoticed (Luke 14:7-10; Mark 10:45; Romans 12:10); being sincere (Matthew 5:37); being discreet in speaking and keeping silence (James 3:10; Matthew 18:15); absence of preoccupation about tomorrow (Matthew 6:32-4); pleasant manner (Matthew 6:16); benevolence (Romans 12:15); punctuality (Matthew 25:1-13; Luke 12:1-16); struggle with indolence and sloth (Matthew 20:1-16); perseverance (Luke 9:62; Matthew 24:13; 25:21).

12. John 10:10.

4: THE UNDERSONG OF JUSTICE

1. Joan Chittister, *Fire in these Ashes* (Gracewing, 1995).
2. Pinchas Lapide, *The Sermon on the Mount – Utopia or Program for Action* (Orbis, 1978).
3. *ibid.*, p. 22.
4. Matthew 6:23.
5. Eric Hobsbawm, *Age of Extremes: The Short Twentieth Century 1914-91* (Abacus, 1995).
6. James Alison, *The Joy of Being Wrong* (Crossroad/Herder, 1998).
7. Pat Clarke told me these stories about his friend Brendan Kennelly.
8. These observations are recorded by Robert Ellsberg in his panoply of modern saints, *All Saints* (Crossroad, 1999).
9. Ephesians 4:13. Some texts are translated that 'We should grow up into the full stature of our humanity, fully mature with the fullness of Christ himself.'
10. Leslie Marmion Silke, *Ceremony*.
11. Hugh Brody, *The Other Side of Eden* (Faber, 2001).
12. The word is *sedakah* – and it is often translated as 'justice'.
13. Lapide, *The Sermon on the Mount*, p. 22.
14. Philip Hallie, *Lest Innocent Blood be Shed* (HarperCollins, 1994).
15. I am not sure of the source, but I think it was in the journal *Cross Currents*, 1984.
16. Matthew 5:6 NJB.
17. Joan Chittister, *A Passion for Life* (Orbis, 1996).
18. Terry Velling, *Living in the Margins* (Crossroad/Herder).
19. The quotations here are from *Living in the Margins*.
20. Luke 16:10 AV.
21. The quotes here come from an article, 'Calling the Shots', by Martin Woollacott in *The Guardian*, 18 January 1994.
22. Matthew 5:44.
23. Matthew 5:43.

5: THE UNDERSONG OF PEACEMAKING

1. Micah 4:3-5.
2. Thomas Merton, *Seeds of Contemplation* (Greenwood Press, 1983).
3. *ibid.*, p. 94.
4. *Sojourners* (August 1979) quotes Einstein in the context of an article on Billy Graham's 'change of heart', and is the source of this observation.
5. Merton, *Seeds of Contemplation*.
6. *ibid*.
7. *ibid*.

6: THE UNDERSONG OF POVERTY

1. Joan Chittister, *A Passion for Life* (Orbis, 1996).
2. Matthew 22:1-14.
3. Annette M. Pellier, 'Misery meets Mystery in Montenegro – A Survival Guide for North American Religious', *Review for Religious*, Vol. 56. No. 6 (Nov.-Dec. 1997).
4. Bill Cook, in conversation at Salem Mass, 1989.
5. I cannot recall how I came upon this story of Robert Coles, but I think I have recorded it correctly.
6. John 1:14.
7. Mark 3:29.
8. Juan Luis Segundo, 'Capitalism versus Socialism: Crux Theologica' in *Frontiers of Theology in Latin America*, ed. R. Gibellini (Orbis).
9. Chittister, *A Passion for Life*.
10. Luke 14:12-24.
11. John 4:31.
12. Matthew 26:29.
13. Luke 6:20.
14. Robert Frost, *Selected Poems* (Penguin, 1973).
15. Wayne Meeks, *God the Economist* (Fortress, 1989).
16. *ibid*.

7: THE UNDERSONG OF PRAYER

1. Etty Hillesum, *An Interrupted Life* (Persephone Books, 1999).
2. Henry David Thoreau, *The Maine Woods* (Penguin, 1988).
3. Dag Hammarskjøld, quoted by Robert Ellsberg in *All Saints* (Crossroad, 1999).
4. Gerard Hughes, *God of Surprises* (Darton, Longman and Todd, 1996).
5. W. Dow Edgerton, *The Passion of Interpretation* (John Knox Press, 1992).
6. Matthew 6:34.
7. Matthew 6:6.
8. Psalm 44.
9. Psalm 91:15.
10. These remarks of Eliezel Bukovitz are quoted by Norman Solomon in 'Theological Trends in Jewish Holocaust Theology', *The Way*, Vol. 37 (July 1997).
11. These and later remarks came from an article in *Sojourners* (October 1990), together with a conversation we had over a few days in 1997.
12. Walter Wink, *Engaging the Powers* (Fortress, 1992).
13. *ibid*.
14. Hillesum, *An Interrupted Life*.
15. Psalm 146:3.

16. Tómas Borgé became the Minister of Justice in the Sandinista government.
17. Gerard Hughes, *In Search of a Way* (Darton, Longman and Todd, 1986).
18. Rainer Maria Rilke, *Selected Poetry of Rainer Maria Rilke* (Picador Classics, 1987).
19. Revelation 21:3-4.

8: THE UNDERSONG OF SUFFERING

1. Psalm 121:2.
2. Yvonne Vera, *Butterfly Burning* (Baobab Books, 1999).
3. Irving Greenberg, quoted in Norman Sullivan, 'Theological Trends: Jewish Holocaust Theology', *The Way*, Vol. 37 No. 3 (July 1997), pp. 242–53.
4. Genesis 17.
5. Martin Israel quotes this in *The Pain that Heals* (Mowbray, 2001) and he acknowledges the permission as from the Sue Ryder Foundation.
6. George Monbiot, 'Hell's Grannies', *The Guardian*, 14 August 2001.
7. *ibid.*
8. Margot Kässmann, 'Moral Formation and Every Day Issues', *The Ecumenical Review*, Vol. 49. No. 3 (July 1997), pp. 366-70.
9. Br Roger of Taizé, *Parable of Community* (Mowbray).

9: THE UNDERSONG OF RECONCILIATION

1. Donald W. Schriver, *An ethic for Enemies: Forgiveness in Politics* (OUP, 1995).
2. Revelation 21:4.
3. Robert Schreiter, *The Ministry of Reconciliation – Spirituality and Strategies* (Orbis, 1998).
4. Colossians 1:20.
5. Colossians 1:16.
6. In the *International Mission Review*,Vol. XXX No. 337, p. 192.
7. Anthony Clare, *The Guardian*.
8. Mark 5:31.
9. Genesis 2:15.
10. Chris Rice, 'Oooh . . . is that racism on your shoe?' *Sojourners* (November/December 2000).
11. Jürgen Moltmann, *The Open Church* (SCM Press).
12. Romans 15:7, 13.
13. Moltmann, *The Open Church*.
14. Barry Lopez, *About this Life – Journeys on the Threshold of Memory* (Panther, 2001).
15. James Alison, *Knowing Jesus* (SPCK, 1998).
16. *ibid.*

17. Ephesians 2:14.
18. Ephesians 2:15 (my own translation).

10: THE UNDERSONG OF LOVE

1. Barry Lopez, *About this Life – Journeys on the Threshold of Memory* (Panther, 2001).
2. Geoffrey Bull, *When Iron Gates Yield* (Hodder and Stoughton).
3. Elie Wiesel, *The Gates of the Forest*, quoted in his autobiography, *All Rivers Run to the Sea* (HarperCollins, 1997).
4. The poem is called 'All of This' and is by Anthony Petrovsky. It was published in *DoubleTake* (Fall, 1998). *DoubleTake* is published by the Center of Documentary Studies at Duke University.
5. Morris L. West, *Shoes of the Fisherman*.
6. Matthew 25:31-46.
7. Ammon Hennacy, quoted in Robert Ellsberg, *All Saints* (Crossroad, 1999).
8. James Alison, *Knowing Jesus* (SPCK, 1998).
9. The quote is from Lynn Rhodes, *Co-Creating: A Feminist View of Ministry* (Westminster, 1987). However, I am grateful for not only this insight, but also those of Robert McAfee Brown, whose delightful little book *Spirituality and Liberation* (Westminster, 1988) was the source.
10. 1 John 4:19.
11. Elie Wiesel, *All Rivers Run to the Sea* (HarperCollins, 1997).
12. Hebrews 7:25.
13. Rainer Maria Rilke, *Selected Poetry of Rainer Maria Rilke* (Picador Classics, 1987).
14. The prayer is of St Richard of Chichester.

UNDERSONG – CADENZA

1. The tune is based on an old Swedish hymn tune and is recorded by Jan Johansson, piano, and George Riedel, bass, on a disc entitled '*Jazz pa svenska*'. Sadly I have not been able to find it on CD.